D1391647

WOMEN
who changed the
WORLD

igloobooks

Published in 2018
by Igloo Books Ltd
Cottage Farm
Sywell
NN6 0BJ
www.igloobooks.com

HUN001 0618
2 4 6 8 10 9 7 5 3 1
ISBN 978-1-78810-452-4

Image credits: Front cover: tl Michael Scott / Alamy Stock Photo;
tr dpa picture alliance / Alamy Stock Photo; bottom row, l-r,
1 Allstar Picture Library / Alamy Stock Photo;
2 Everett Collection Inc / Alamy Stock Photo;
3 Ian Dagnall / Alamy Stock Photo;
4 Lionel Cherruault Royal Picture Library / Alamy Stock Photo;
5 peter jordan / Alamy Stock Photo
All other imagery: © iStock / Getty Images

Written by Carrie Lewis

Designed by Nicholas Gage
Edited by Bobby Newlyn-Jones

Printed and manufactured in China

Contents

Introduction

'A woman is like a tea bag: you never know how strong she is until you put her in hot water.'

This quote comes from Eleanor Roosevelt, a woman who saw her fair share of 'hot water' and one of the many wise and talented women who grace the pages that follow.

At the heart of her quote is the idea that women as a whole are, to some degree, unknown or not yet fully explored; the best of them is not discovered until they are challenged.

The women described on the following pages have all faced considerable challenges: challenges of gender or restrictions of society; challenges as a result disability, illness or poverty. Some have faced prison for their beliefs and perhaps all have fought against the disbelief that women are capable of achieving extraordinary things.

Take, for example, Frida Kahlo, a woman from a poor country with a lifelong disability, whose art has astonished the world; or Margaret Sanger who was so devoted to the cause of birth control that she went to prison for it; or take Serena Williams, a brilliant sportswoman whose passion and drive for life has redefined the notion of femininity.

Not all of these women would consider themselves to be feminists, or world-changers. Some, like Barbara Hepworth or Amelia Earhart, merely want to get on with their jobs and let their talent be seen. For others, changing the role and status of women has been an important motivational force: like the suffragettes or feminist writer Betty Friedan.

Above: American humanitarian and social activist, Eleanor Roosevelt

'Women must try to do things as men have tried. When they fail, their failure must be but a challenge to others.'

Amelia Earhart

Introduction

These women come from all stages of history and all ranks of society. Remarkable women are not a new phenomenon, they have always been with us but somewhere amidst the necessities of motherhood and the acceptance of patriarchy, their stories and skills have been overlooked. Women's lives are the great untold history of civilisation.

On reading the story of each woman that follows, perhaps consider the millions of women whose skills and courage have been lost along the way; stories untold and aspirations never realised. Then marvel at the stories that are here, made all the more precious by their rarity.

Below: Lady Diana Spencer became loved and respected for her passionate involvement with a number of charities, both at home and worldwide

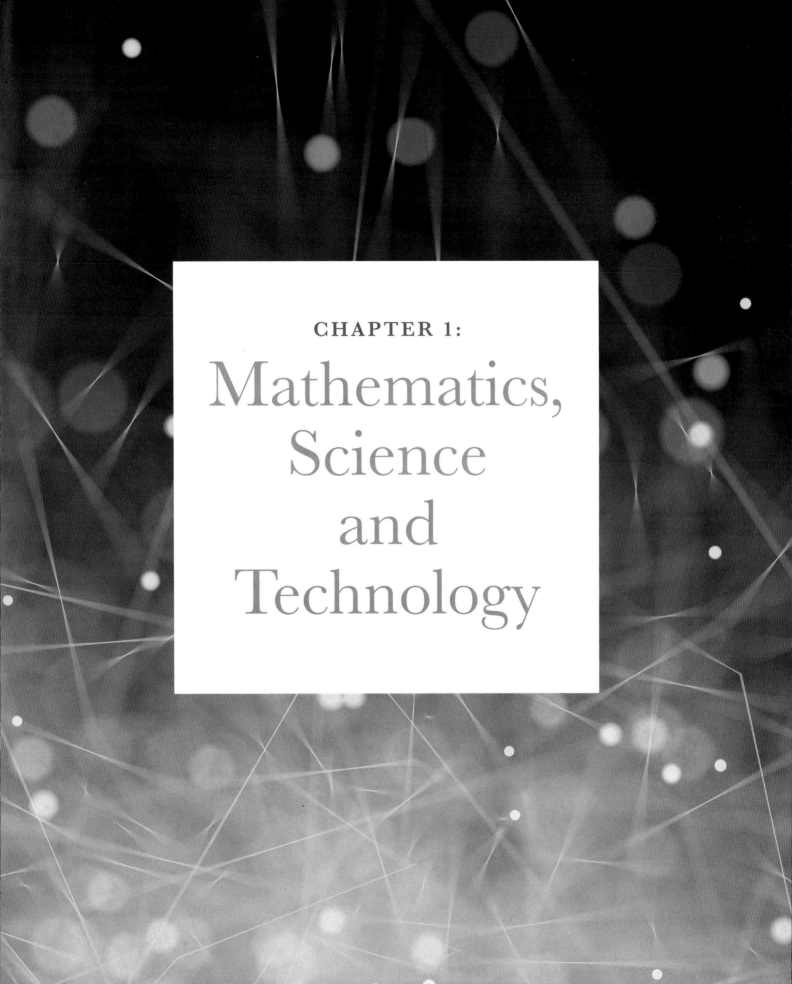

CHAPTER 1:
Mathematics, Science and Technology

Mathematics, Science and Technology

Clara Barton

1821–1912 | American | Nurse

Clara Barton was a teacher and lecturer and a nurse who helped wounded soldiers on the battlefield during the American Civil War. She is most well known, however, as the founder of the American Red Cross. Courageous and dedicated to a life of serving others, Barton was known as the 'Angel of the Battlefield' for the direct part she played in relieving wounded soldiers.

As a child, Barton found her calling when she nursed her brother back to health after he was hurt in an accident. She became a teacher and later opened her own school.

When the American Civil War started in 1861, Barton wanted to help the Union Army and started by distributing supplies, but quickly moved into nursing, first working directly on a battlefield in 1862. After the war she worked in the War Office helping soldiers to find their families again.

In 1870, Barton visited Europe and helped the International Red Cross during the Franco-Russian War. On her return to the USA she was determined to set up a similar organisation at home. When the American Red Cross was founded in 1881, Barton served as its first President and oversaw relief work for the Galveston and Johnstown floods. She continued working and lecturing almost until her death in 1912, and wrote her autobiography, *The Story of my Childhood*, in 1907.

Clara Barton, nurse, educator and founder of the American Red Cross

Mathematics, Science and Technology

Elizabeth Blackwell

1821–1910 | British | Doctor

At a time when women were lucky to receive a good education, let alone pursue a career, Elizabeth Blackwell found a way to qualify and practise as a doctor. Fighting prejudice all her life, Blackwell applied to every medical school she could think of, asking to be allowed to study there. When accepted at Geneva Medical College in New York, the college initially accepted her as a joke. Blackwell called their bluff, however, by qualifying as an MD in 1849 – the first woman to achieve this distinction.

Born in Bristol, England, into a family who moved to the USA in order to fight slavery, Blackwell was not new to the idea of prejudice and oppression. She wasn't initially drawn to the idea of a medical career, but became so after the death of a close friend. She engaged friends to help her find out how to pursue a medical career and although most people believed it impossible for her to train as a doctor, her determined attitude eventually prevailed. Following her epic fight to qualify, it was a further struggle to find a job. Eventually, however, she found work in London and Paris, and studied midwifery before returning to the USA.

With the help of her sister and Dr Marie Zakrzewska, Blackwell opened the New York Infirmary for Women and Children in 1857 to care for the poor of New York. After several years they were also able to offer training and experience to women who wished to work in medicine.

Although her health declined in later years, Blackwell fought until the end of her life for the reform of women's rights and better access to female medical staff for women who wanted to be seen by female physicians. She paved the way for the equality that today is evidenced in the medical community.

Elizabeth Blackwell, the first woman to receive a medical degree in the US

Mathematics, Science and Technology

Marie Curie

1867–1934 | Polish/French | Physicist

The dangers of radiation were not understood in the early days of research
and Marie Curie almost certainly died from its effects

Mathematics, Science and Technology

Marie Curie was a distinguished chemist and physicist and the winner of two Nobel Prizes. A pioneer for women in science, her brilliance was so extreme that no prejudice against women could obscure it. She formulated the theory of radioactivity. Her achievements were all the more remarkable because she had to struggle against prejudices that barred women from studying at the highest levels around the turn of the 19th and 20th centuries.

Born Maria Skłodowska in Poland in 1867, Marie Curie demonstrated exceptional intellectual abilities from an early age, but was unable to pursue her education after the age of 18 because her family could not afford it. She worked as a governess for two years in order to finance her sister's medical studies, on the understanding that she would do the same for her.

In 1891, Curie moved to Paris where she studied physics, chemistry and mathematics at the Sorbonne, earning a degree in mathematics in 1894. She intended to return to work in Poland, but when she was denied a place at Krakow University because she was a woman, she returned to Paris where she married fellow scientist Pierre Curie in 1895. Pierre Curie specialised in the electrical and magnetic properties of crystals, which is the area of study that first drew the Curies together. Marie Curie also worked under the guidance of the scientist Henri Becquerel, who had discovered that uranium emitted unusual rays.

Curie performed a series of experiments to establish that the uranium atoms emit an energy, which she termed 'radiation', and used an electrometer invented by her husband to discover that the air around uranium was a low-level conductor of electricity. This was the beginning of the Curies' research into the properties of radiation and the start of their experiments to isolate elements that were naturally radioactive. By 1898, they had discovered two new elements, which they named polonium (in honour of Marie's native land) and radium (because of its intense radioactivity). In 1903, Curie was awarded her doctorate and in the

Marie Curie separated radium from its surrounding radioactive residues in sufficient quantities for other scientists to study

same year, along with Becquerel and her husband Pierre, won the Nobel Prize for Physics for their joint work on spontaneous radiation.

Marie Curie's greatest achievement was to separate radium from its surrounding radioactive residues in sufficient quantities for scientist to study its properties. She also worked to stockpile radioactive elements for the purpose of research into their medicinal uses and for research into nuclear physics.

Despite the sudden death of Pierre Curie in 1906 in a traffic accident, Marie Curie continued her work and was appointed his professorship one month after his death – the first female professor at the Sorbonne. She published the first serious article on radium in 1910 and the following year was awarded an unprecedented second Nobel Prize, this time for chemistry.

For many years, Curie worked extremely hard in difficult circumstances, in ill-equipped laboratories, using substances that were to prove damaging to her health. Her notebooks remain so radioactive that they are stored in lead-lined boxes. Her fame after 1911 enabled her to encourage the French government to fund the Radium Institute at the University of Paris. From 1922 she focused on finding practical medical applications for radioactivity.

Curie died in 1934, almost certainly from an illness that resulted from her long exposure to radiation. Her discoveries were immensely important and shaped the work of subsequent scientists in splitting the atom and in using radium to treat cancers.

Above: Madame Curie experimenting at the University of Paris

Right: Marie Curie at the time of her Nobel Prize for chemistry

For many years, Curie worked extremely hard in difficult circumstances, in ill-equipped laboratories, using substances that were to prove damaging to her health.

Amelia Earhart

1897–1937 | American | Aviator

'Women must try to do things as men have tried. When they fail, their failure must be but a challenge to others.'
Amelia Earhart

These words neatly sum up one of Amelia Earhart's fundamental beliefs; that women should challenge all boundaries and show that they were not 'bred to timidity'. Her life was taken up in taking risks and ignoring the fear that came with them. She blazed a trail for women to be leaders, not followers, in adventure.

Born in 1897, Earhart started life in her grandfather's comfortable home in Atchison, Kansas, where she had an unusual degree of freedom for rough, outdoor play. Earhart's parents believed that girls should be equal to boys and later supported Earhart's unusual career.

Earhart's determined belief that women should not appear weaker than men showed itself early: she kept a scrapbook of women who had succeeded in a male-dominated world and clearly wanted to make her mark in a similar way. It was not until 1920, when she had a ride in an aeroplane for the first time, that a career as a pilot became her goal. She worked at several jobs to save money for flying lessons from Neta Snook, a pioneer female aviator, and then later for a plane of her own.

Above: Amelia Earhart smiles upon arriving in London, having become the first woman to fly across the Atlantic alone

Mathematics, Science and Technology

In 1928 came a phone call that changed Earhart's life. It was a phone call from a Captain Railey, who wanted to know if she would like to be the first woman to fly across the Atlantic. Earhart accepted. The project was organised in the wake of Charles Lindbergh's first solo flight over the Atlantic the previous year. Earhart took part in the flight, but frustratingly could not pilot the plane as she hadn't received the right instrument training; a fact that clearly annoyed her, as she compared her role to that of 'a sack of potatoes'.

In 1932, Earhart's wish to fly the Atlantic alone was granted when she became the first woman, and second person ever, to fly across the Atlantic. She set off from Newfoundland on 20th May, scheduled to land in Paris a day later. Forced off course by poor weather, she actually landed in Londonderry in Northern Ireland, to the significant surprise of the locals.

Upon returning to the USA, Earhart was awarded the Distinguished Flying Cross. She began to set records, becoming the first woman to fly solo across the USA and the first woman to fly from Hawaii to the US mainland. She also set records for altitude flying and helped to found the 'Ninety-Nines', an organisation of female pilots.

In 1937, Earhart began the biggest challenge of her life; a round-the-world flight. No one, man or woman, had ever achieved this before. She took off from Oakland, California, on 1st June with navigator Fred Noonan on an Eastbound circumnavigation of the globe in a twin-engine Lockheed 10E Electra. They covered 22,000 miles of the 29,000 mile journey, flying down through South America, then across to Africa and Southeast Asia.

They reached New Guinea on 29th June and prepared for the most difficult part of the journey, the landing on tiny Howard Island to refuel. They were well supported by the Coast Guard anchored off Howard Island, but lost radio concert as they were crossing the Pacific. In spite of one of the largest searches ever, Earhart and Noonan were never seen again, but she had known and accepted the risk she was taking:

'…decide…whether or not the goal is worth the risks involved. If it is, stop worrying….'

Above: Amelia Earhart stands in front of her bi-plane 'Friendship' in Newfoundland

Mathematics, Science and Technology

Gertrude Belle Elion

1918–1999 | American | Medicine

Nobel Prize winner Gertrude Belle Elion made giant strides in the world of medicine. By studying the chemistry of diseased cells, Elion and her colleagues devised medicines to combat leukaemia, AIDs, herpes and many other diseases. They also helped to prevent organ rejection in kidney transplant patients. Many thousands of people around the world have benefited from Elion's hard work, innovation and compassion.

Born in New York City and raised in the Bronx, Elion was motivated to work in medical science by the death of her grandfather from cancer when she was 15. She excelled at school and went to study at Hunter College in New York, graduating at the age of 19. Jobs in chemistry were hard to come by, however, until World War II, when women were called upon to do jobs previously done by men. In 1944, Elion went to work with Dr George Hitchings at Burroughs Wellcome (now GlaxoSmithKline). The two formed a forty-year partnership in which Hitchings granted Elion wider responsibility in light of her ability. By the end of her career, Elion had 43 patents for new medicines.

Elion never married and was very driven by her work, but had many hobbies and led a happy and fulfilled life. In 1991, she was awarded the Nobel Prize for her achievements, alongside Dr Hitchings. In the same year, she became the first woman to be inducted into the National Inventors Hall of Fame.

Above: American biochemist and pharmacologist, Gertrude Belle Elion, co-winner of the 1988 Nobel Prize for Medicine

'I had no specific bent toward science until my grandfather died of cancer. I decided nobody should suffer that much.'

Gertrude Belle Elion

Mathematics, Science and Technology

Anne McLaren

1927–2007 | British | IVF Treatment

For centuries, the inability to have children has caused enormous distress to couples. Anne McLaren's discoveries and research into fertility paved the way to finding a solution to this that has proved life-changing for thousands of people: the 'miracle' of in vitro fertilisation, or IVF.

Born in London and the daughter of a baron, McLaren spent her war years as a child at the family estate in Wales. She went to study zoology at Oxford, continuing her postgraduate studies at University College London where she also met her husband, Donald Michie. Her research at UCL was mainly conducted on mice, some of which focused on the fertility of mice.

McLaren moved to Edinburgh University to continue her work in 1955, and in 1958 she made a breakthrough in her research when a litter of mice was born from embryos that had been grown inside a test tube and then transferred to a surrogate mother. She continued to research fertility and the development of embryos including the creation of 'chimeras', or animals made of cells that come from two distinct zygotes, or fertilised eggs. In 1974, she moved back to UCL as director of the Medical Research Council's Mammalian Development Unit. McLaren retired in 1992, but co-founded the Frozen Ark, a repository of genetic material from endangered animals to be used for research purposes.

Although McLaren and Michie remained amicable throughout their lives, the couple divorced in 1959 and McLaren raised their three children largely as a single parent. This led to her strong advocacy of the need for childcare provision for working women.

McLaren died in a car accident in 2007, but the significance of her work has been felt in many areas, not least in the development of human in vitro fertilisation.

Above: A portrait of Dame Anne McLaren by artist Emma Wesley, which is owned by the Royal Society

McLaren's groundbreaking work led to significant advancements, including IVF therapy and the preservation of cells from endangered animals.

Rosalind Franklin

1920–1958 | British | DNA Research

Once called the 'dark lady' of DNA, Rosalind Franklin's contribution towards our understanding of the structure of DNA was partly obscured at first, when some of her research was used by others without her permission. Her untimely death also meant that she was unable to tell her own story. Others, however, have taken it upon themselves to bring her work to light. One prominent scientist, John Desmond Bernal, spoke highly of Franklin at the time of her death: 'As a scientist, Miss Franklin was distinguished by extreme clarity and perfection in everything she undertook.'

Born in 1920 into a wealthy London family, Franklin's intelligence was obvious from an early age and by the time she was 15 she knew that she wanted to be a scientist. When she was 18, she enrolled at Newnham College, Cambridge, to study chemistry and continued her studies to complete a PhD in 1945 with a study into the porosity of coal.

An important development in Franklin's career came in 1946, when she went to work in Paris with crystallographer Jacques Mering. He taught Franklin X-ray diffraction, a technique which proved vital to her later work photographing the structure of DNA. Franklin pioneered the use of X-rays to create images of crystallised solids in unorganised matter.

On returning to Britain, Franklin went to work with John Randall at Kings College, London, who used her expertise in X-ray diffraction techniques to study DNA fibres. The images that Franklin produced were so clear that they offered new insights into the structure of DNA; she discovered that DNA had two forms, the A or 'dry' form, and the B or 'wet' form. One of her photographs of the B form, known as photograph 51, became an essential part of the study to discover the structure of DNA.

The photo was the result of 100 hours of exposure on a machine refined by Franklin herself. Franklin was known in scientific circles for her extreme diligence and the care she exercised over every stage of the processes she undertook. The success of photograph 51 is in large part owing to Franklin's efforts to refine the machine, monitor the exposure and develop the photograph to perfection. Unfortunately for her, however, a quarrel with her colleague Maurice Wilkins meant that the photograph was disclosed to Francis Crick and James Watson at Cambridge University without her knowledge. Crick and Watson were also studying DNA and photograph 51 was a tremendous breakthrough for them.

Watson said, on seeing the photograph, 'My jaw fell open, my heart began to race'. Crick and Watson published their model of DNA in March 1953, and later on in 1962 were awarded the Nobel Prize for it. Franklin's boss, John Randall, came to an agreement with Cambridge University that Franklin and Wilkins should be acknowledged for the significance of their work with regards to Watson and Crick's success and their work was eventually published together, but Crick and Watson still retained the majority of the credit for the work. Franklin left the lab in 1953 and never complained publicly about the use of her material without permission.

Franklin was diagnosed with cancer at the age of 36 and died in 1958. She continued working until just weeks before her death, leaving behind her a muted legacy in a scientific field with which many might still be unfamiliar.

Right: Chemist and crystallographer, Rosalind Franklin, is best known for her role in the discovery of the structure of DNA

Right: The Rosalind Franklin Building at Newnham College, Cambridge, acts as both memorial and as student accommodation

Mathematics, Science and Technology

Margaret Hamilton

Born 1936 | American | Computer Scientist

A true pioneer of the space age, Margaret Hamilton was an essential part of the first moon landing, owing to her work in software engineering. A brilliant mathematician and creative thinker, Hamilton was a leader in the early stages of software development.

Born Margaret Heafield in 1936, Hamilton first studied maths and philosophy at Richmond College, Indiana. After a spell as a teacher during the early years of her marriage while her husband was at Harvard Law School, she went to work for MIT, where she began programming software to predict the weather. Not long after, she went to work in MIT's Lincoln Laboratory, initially on software to detect enemy aircraft, then in the 1960s, she led a team that worked on the guidance and control systems for the Apollo mission.

Since all of this was new technology, the team had to think a lot of things through from scratch. Hamilton herself focused on developing software to detect system errors and information recovery after system crashes. Both of these things were critical to the famous Apollo 11 mission in which Neil Armstrong and Buzz Aldrin first walked on the moon.

In the 1970s, Hamilton left MIT to work in the private sector, and in 1986 became the CEO of Hamilton Technologies. She has published over 130 papers about her work and was presented with the Presidential Medal of Freedom in 2016. She was also given NASA's Exceptional Space Act Award in 2003.

Above: NASA mathematician and computer software pioneer Margaret Hamilton before being awarded the Presidential Medal of Freedom by US President, Barack Obama

Hamilton's work in software engineering included guidance and control systems for the Apollo mission, resulting in the success of the first moon landing.

Mathematics, Science and Technology

Sally Ride

1951–2012 | American | Astronaut and Physicist

Above: Third woman in space, and first American woman, Sally Ride in a NASA shirt with a logo of the Challenger Space Shuttle STS-7 mission

Science and space exploration have perhaps proved two of the most difficult areas for women to make their mark, but a few women have managed to succeed. In the US, one of the most successful and high profile female scientists in the field was Sally Ride. The first American woman in space, Ride not only made a successful career as an astronaut and physicist, but went on to develop and encourage the next generation of scientists with her work in education.

Ride was born in 1951 and grew up in Los Angeles. She attended Stanford University to study physics and English, continuing beyond her degree to take a master's and a PhD, completing her studies in 1978. In the same year, Ride applied for a place on the Astronaut programme at NASA and was selected from over 1000 applicants to take a place.

After years of rigorous training, Ride finally got her chance to go into space in June 1983 on the Challenger space shuttle. Although men had been going into space for over a decade, Ride was the first woman to do so. She took an important role on the space shuttle as a mission specialist and remained in space for six days. The following October, Ride returned to space as a mission specialist, again on Challenger. She was scheduled to make a third space flight, but it was cancelled after the Challenger shuttle tragedy in 1986, in which several astronauts died. Ride was part of the team that investigated the tragedy in the aftermath.

After leaving NASA, Ride became the director of the California Space Institute at the University of California and founded her own company, Sally Ride Science, to inspire women and young girls to pursue careers in science.

'For whatever reason, I didn't succumb to the stereotype that science wasn't for girls. I got encouragement from my parents. I never ran into a teacher or a counselor who told me that science was for boys. A lot of my friends did.'

Sally Ride

Grace Hopper

1906–1992 | American | USN Rear Admiral

Grace Hopper's legacy isn't made up of words, it speaks to us from her actions. She stands not only for brilliance, but also for determination. Judged too old and too thin to be in the US Navy, she served for forty years and ended her life a Rear Admiral. At a time when women didn't do mathematics and computers were unheard of, she excelled in both. The first woman to graduate in maths from Yale University, she was later became a pioneer of the digital age. Hopper was so effective and unique in her skills that the Navy would not let her retire and kept recalling her for active duty even when she was over 70.

Born Grace Brewster Murray in New York City on 9th December 1906, Hopper studied mathematics at Yale University, where she earned a master's degree. The same year, she married Vincent Foster Hopper, becoming Grace Hopper (a name that she kept even after the couple's 1945 divorce). She went on to take a PhD in mathematics – the first woman to do so.

Hopper worked as a lecturer until World War II, when she sought to enlist in the US Navy, but was not allowed owing to her age and small stature. Instead, she went to the US Reserves and was commissioned as a lieutenant in June 1944. Given her mathematical background, Hopper was assigned to the Bureau of Ordnance Computation Project at Harvard University, where she learned to program a Mark I computer.

After the war, Hopper remained with the Navy as a reserve officer and continued to work in special computing projects. She worked with the Mark II and Mark III computers and was at Harvard when a moth was found to have shorted out the Mark II, leading to the coining of the term 'computer bug'.

Hopper moved into private industry in 1949, first with the Eckert-Mauchly Computer Corporation, then with Remington Rand where she oversaw programming for the UNIVAC computer. In 1952, her team created the first compiler for computer languages (a compiler renders worded instructions into code that can be read by computers). This compiler was a precursor for the Common Business Oriented Language, or COBOL, a widely adapted language that would be used around the world.

Above: Grace Murray Hopper's first love was the US Navy

Left: Commodore Grace Hopper in her office

Mathematics, Science and Technology

Hopper retired from the Naval Reserve in 1966, but her pioneering computer work meant that she was recalled to active duty at the age of 60 to tackle standardising communication between different computer languages. When she retired in 1986, at age 79, she was a Rear Admiral as well as the oldest serving officer in the service.

At a time when most people her age would be glad to put their feet up, Hopper took yet another job and stayed in the computer industry for several more years. She was awarded the National Medal of Technology in 1991, becoming the first female individual recipient of the honour. At the age of 85, she died in Arlington, Virginia, on 1st January 1992 and was laid to rest in the Arlington National Cemetery.

After her death, Hopper continued to inspire. In 1997, the guided missile destroyer, USS Hopper, was named in her honour and in 2004, the University of Missouri honoured Hopper with a computer museum on their campus, dubbed 'Grace's Place'. In 2016, Hopper was posthumously honoured with the Presidential Medal of Freedom by Barack Obama.

With regards to her manner of operating, Hopper is noted as once saying that:

'If it's a good idea, go ahead and do it. It's much easier to apologize than it is to get permission.'

Above: Lieutenant Grace Hopper codes problems onto punch tape for feeding into a new calculating machine

Mathematics, Science and Technology

Ada Lovelace

1815–1852 | British | Mathematics

At a time when women were not often educated in mathematics, Ada Lovelace's natural ability with numbers and coding, as well as her sheer determination to learn, made her one of the first people to write instructions for a computer program, even before the existence of computers as we know them.

Her father was the famous poet Lord Byron who, whilst brilliant, was also moody and notoriously eccentric. His marriage to Lovelace's mother, Lady Anne Byron, ended shortly after Lovelace was born. She never saw her father again.

Lovelace's mother believed that giving her daughter an education in science and mathematics would make her less likely to inherit her father's stranger characteristics (or 'insanity', as she called it), and she found tutors to encourage Lovelace's natural intellectual gifts. One of these was Mary Somerville, a Scottish mathematician and astronomer who was one of the first women to be admitted to the Royal Astronomical Society.

In the course of her studies, Lovelace met many great intellectuals of the day and at the age of 17 she met Charles Babbage, an inventor and mathematician who became her mentor and proved to be a hugely important figure in her later achievements.

At 20, Lovelace married William King, who became the Earl of Lovelace and gave her the name by which she is best known. They had three children together and surprisingly for the times, King encouraged her studies throughout their marriage, although by the time Ada died, the pair were estranged.

As a married woman, Lovelace continued her work with Charles Babbage. He invented plans for a 'Difference Engine' for performing calculations and later also created plans for something he called an 'Analytical Engine', which could perform even more complex calculations. Both of these devices were effectively prototype computers. When Lovelace saw the Analytical Engine, she was fascinated by the possibilities that it created.

Babbage's work was scrutinised by other scientists, among them an Italian mathematician called Luigi Menabrea, who wrote an article on the proposed Analytical Engine. Lovelace, who was also a gifted linguist, translated the article from French to English and at the same time appended a significant number of her own notes on the use of the Analytical Engine. In her notes, she included an algorithm for how the engine could be used to find Bernoulli numbers, a series of rational numbers which occur in number theory. It is considered to be the first ever published algorithm specifically tailored for implementation on a computer and for this reason, Ada Lovelace has often been cited as the first computer programmer. Her notes for using the engine were in fact three times longer than the original article and the translation with the notes was published in the journal Scientific Memoirs under the initials AAL.

Unlike Babbage and Menabrea, Lovelace was convinced that the Analytical Engine could be used for functions beyond mere calculation:

[The Analytical Engine] might act upon other things besides number ... Supposing, for instance, that the fundamental relations of pitched sounds in the science of harmony and of musical composition were susceptible of such expression and adaptations, the engine might compose elaborate and scientific pieces of music of any degree of complexity or extent.

Lovelace died at the age of just 36. Her work was forgotten for a while, but was rediscovered when it was republished by BV Bowden in 1953, when its significance in the development of computers aroused renewed interest. The 'Lovelace Medal' is now an award given to women who excel in the field of computing and 'Ada' is the name given to the computer language used by the US Defense Department.

Florence Nightingale

1820–1910 | English | Nurse

It is impossible to estimate the lives that have been saved by Nightingale's work. Her legacy lives in all of us, from the expectations we have for our own healthcare to her life-saving standards of nursing and hygiene.

Florence Nightingale was born at a time when well-off women, like herself, were expected to marry and become respectable wives, but she had other ideas. She wanted a life that was useful and considered nursing to be her true calling. Finally, at the age of 30, having turned down the proposal of long-term suitor Richard Milnes, she was allowed to leave home and went to study nursing in Germany. In Britain at the time, nursing was largely unregulated and considered a menial role to be carried out by amateurs. In 1853, Nightingale became Superintendent in a London hospital, and set out to make things better.

In 1854, British soldiers were fighting the Crimean War near the Black Sea to the south of Russia. Nightingale led a team of 38 nurses to Scutari in the Crimea to aid the treatment of the injured soldiers. Conditions were terrible; rat infested, insanitary hospitals meant that infection was rife. At first, the soldiers made worse recoveries in the hospital than they did out of it. To improve matters, Nightingale organised a thorough cleaning of the hospital, engaging the help of the least infirm patients as well as the nurses, and also organised a laundry so that clean linen could be provided. By improving sanitation in the hospital, Nightingale reduced the death rate by two thirds. She also improved the quality of food and began a library so that recovering patients could entertain themselves.

Nightingale was known as 'The Lady of the Lamp', a description which makes her sound gentle and angelic. In fact, although she was dedicated to her patients, Nightingale was brisk and business-like in her manner and did not suffer fools gladly.

On her return home from Scutari, Nightingale was amazed to find herself considered a hero. She was awarded a financial prize as well as an engraved brooch by Queen Victoria, by way of thanks. Her fame also made the profession of nursing much more respectable and well-off girls from good families began signing up for nursing careers.

Above: nurse and hospital reformer, Florence Nightingale, in old age

Right: Florence Nightingale during the time she was tending to the wounded during the Crimean War, Russia, circa 1855

Mathematics, Science and Technology

To research the spread of disease, Nightingale used mathematical and statistical methods and invented the polar-area diagram, a system similar to a pie chart that she used to calculate the number of soldiers who died or recovered. In 1858, she provided a huge report on her experiences of healthcare in Scutari, to be used in further field hospitals and on the containment of infection in general. In the American Civil War, Nightingale was frequently consulted on the running of field hospitals and her advice was often needed on a wide range of nursing and hygiene issues in both army and civilian hospitals.

In 1860, Nightingale founded St Thomas' Hospital in London and within it a training school called the Nightingale Training School for Nurses. This was the beginning of the modern nursing profession.

When Nightingale was 38, she began to suffer seriously from an illness contracted in the Crimea called brucellosis, which largely confined her to her bed. Never work-shy, Nightingale continued to act, from her bed, as a consultant and adviser on matters of nursing until her death in 1913.

Left: A memorial to and statue of Florence Nightingale, Central London

Bletchley Park Code Breakers

1938–1945 | England | Code Breakers

During World War II, a huge secret code-breaking operation at Bletchley Park in Buckinghamshire was instrumental in bringing the war to a successful end. The operation intercepted secret information that the Germans were sending to troops and allies using their Enigma machine. The Bletchley Park operators also learned to send false information, including false information about D-Day, back to the Germans. This enabled the Allies to discover what the Germans were planning and conceal their own operations.

Although it was rare at the time for women to be educated to degree standard as linguists and mathematicians, the shortage of available young men (many were away fighting) meant that those recruiting for Bletchley Park had to cast the net wide. People were recruited to work at Bletchley Park from universities and the armed forces, but also in more imaginative ways: through crossword and chess competitions.

At the height of its activities, Bletchley Park employed around 12,000 people, around 75 per cent of whom were women. Many of these women operated the code-breaking machines or 'bombes', some were administrators or dispatch riders and some were translators and code breakers. They were all sworn to secrecy to such an extent that many of their actions have only recently become known.

Here are four women who were part of the successful operation at Bletchley Park.

Below: The Mansion in Bletchley Park, where the codebreaking began in 1938

Mavis Batey (1921–2013)

Mavis Batey was one of the top code breakers at Bletchley Park. A German linguist who studied at University College London, she was recruited to work for Dilly Knox at Bletchley Park at the age of 19. She was instrumental in cracking Enigma, the German coding machine that many thought could never be broken.

Batey became so proficient at decoding messages that she could recognise individual styles of enemy operators of Enigma. Her finest hour came when she cracked a code enciphered by the Italian Navy detailing their plans to attack a British food convoy from Egypt to Greece. The British Navy were informed of the planned attack and turned the tables, attacking first. The Italian Navy never engaged the British Navy again.

Joan Clarke (1917–1996)

Joan Clarke was a gifted mathematician who was recruited from Cambridge University to work in GCCS, (the Government Code and Cipher School). She worked in Hut 8, decoding ciphers throughout the war, and eventually became deputy head of the section, although she was never paid as much as her male colleagues. In recognition of her work, she was eventually awarded the grade of 'linguist', although she spoke no foreign languages; it was the only way to be paid the amount that she was worth. Joan was briefly engaged to Alan Turing, the famous programmer and mathematician, and the two remained friends until his death in 1954.

Margaret Rock (1903–1983)

Margaret Rock, like Mavis Batey, was employed by Dilly Knox in the code-breaking section. She helped to decode messages sent in code by the Enigma machine. She was considered one of the finest code breakers in the section and was promoted to senior cryptographer. After the war, she continued to work in secret governmental posts, such as GCHQ (Government Communications Headquarters).

Ruth Briggs (1920–2005)

Ruth Briggs, a modern languages graduate from Cambridge, was a linguist and an expert German speaker. She worked on Z watch at Bletchley Park, translating the messages from German to English as they were decoded.

Below and right: former 'Wrens' and Colossus operators reunite at The National Museum of Computing, Bletchley, June 2016

Marie Stopes

1880–1958 | British | Family Planning

Marie Stopes was a campaigner and advocate of family planning and birth control, who established the first family planning clinics in Britain. Her work and writing did much to break down the taboos surrounding sex and contraception and helped to bring liberation to women who had struggled with repeated pregnancies and poor levels of education about sex.

Born in Edinburgh, Stopes initially trained as a palaeobotanist, gaining degrees from University College, London and the University of Munich. In 1904, she became the first female lecturer in science to be appointed to the staff of Manchester University, before spending 18 months in 1907–1908 on a scientific mission to Japan in order to explore and lecture about fossils.

Stopes married Reginald Ruggles Gates in 1911 but it was the failure of this union, which Stopes claimed had been unconsummated, that led her in a completely new direction – that of family planning. The failure of the marriage, which she ascribed to ignorance about sexual matters and contraception, inspired her to write her first book on the subject, *Married Love*, which was published amid considerable controversy in 1918. The book was initially banned in the USA when it was first published.

Other books followed, such as *Wise Parenthood*, also published in 1918, *Contraception: Its Theory, History and Practice* (1923), *Radiant Motherhood* (1920), *Sex and the Young* (1926) and *Sex and Religion* (1929). In total, she published some 70 books on the subject of sex between 1918 and her death in 1958.

Her second marriage in 1918 to Humphrey Verdon Roe was more successful, with a son being born in 1924. Along with her husband, she opened Britain's first family planning clinic in Holloway, London in March 1921. This clinic offered free advice and provision of different methods of contraception to married women. The Mothers' Clinic, as the establishment was known, moved to central London in 1925.

Above and left: Scottish suffragette and advocate of birth control, Dr Marie Stopes

Mathematics, Science and Technology

This was the first of a number of clinics that were established. Stopes herself was opposed to abortion, regarding any means of removing an embryo as murder, and considered birth control through information and contraception the best and only justifiable means of controlling pregnancy. Although the original clinic business was forced into receivership in 1975, it was reformed the following year and today the Marie Stopes International organisation has some 450 clinics worldwide. The clinics today do perform safe abortions, with advice, to women who feel abortion is their best option.

Apart from offering pioneering treatment, The Mothers' Clinic was also at the forefront of research into contraception. It was this work, along with that of other pioneers, that helped to break down the lack of knowledge regarding sexual relationships.

Controversy was always part of Stopes's career and this was particularly true of her belief in eugenics; a philosophy in which the genetic pool is 'purified' by refusing those people who are 'feeble minded' or disabled the right to procreate. This belief was fashionable in intellectual circles at the time and Stopes supported it emphatically in her writing: advocating for some kind of genetic 'utopia'.

Such was her belief in this theory that she disinherited her own son when he married the partially sighted daughter of the scientist Barnes Wallis. Following her death, much of her estate was passed to the Eugenics Society.

Right: Dr Marie Stopes with her husband, Humphrey Verdon Roe, outside the Royal Academy in London

CHAPTER 2:

Literature, Fashion and the Arts

Jane Austen

1775–1817 | British | Author

Jane Austen's novels, though few, have become a treasured feature of the English literary landscape. Serialised for TV and made into films, the stories have been discovered anew by each generation, either as required school reading, holiday paperback or essential viewing. The novels themselves bring to light Austen's shrewd sense of humour, as well as her powers of observation. They also provide interesting insight into the lives and attitudes of 18th-century women.

Austen's female characters are not the stereotypical, glamorous heroines of many novels written in Austen's era. They are believable, living characters with faults as well as feelings. Emma Woodhouse is a gossip and a schemer, although lovable; whilst Elizabeth Bennet is rebellious and sharp-tongued. Often the appeal of the characters lies in the fact that the reader can identify with them. Critics have observed that Austen was good at using speech in her texts to represent thoughts as well as words. This is used to good effect to draw us towards the characters and helps us to understand their complex inner worlds.

Austen's novels also provide a subtle criticism of the way women of the era were forced to live their lives; with little power over finance or work, they were often handed from their birth families to their marital families with little room for their own opinions and heavily restricted by convention and social mores. Austen made this observation in *Northanger Abbey*, possibly a vexed reflection on her own experience:

A woman, especially if she have the misfortune of knowing anything, should conceal it as well as she can.

In *Pride and Prejudice*, Austen famously illustrates the formality and convention associated with the choosing of a mate by members of the gentry. Marriages in Austen's day were less about a love match than a socially expedient match. Austen herself, although never married, was a great believer in love.

As regards Austen's own life, it's possible to see how it was shaped and restrained by social convention. Growing up in Hampshire, Austen is said to have lived happily in her large family, although there is not much documentary evidence to support this. Many of the letters Austen wrote in her life were destroyed, particularly to her sister, supposedly owing to their scathing and sarcastic content. It's therefore impossible to say exactly how Austen felt about her life circumstances. We can, however, speculate that Austen was not considered a desirable marriage partner because she came from a family with no money and she remained single. She did briefly accept a proposal of marriage from Harris Bigg-Wither, supposedly out of convenience, but she turned it down the following day having seemingly admitted to herself that she did not love him.

When Austen's father died, it was left to her brothers to provide an income for herself, her mother and her sister Cassandra, at least until a little money came in from Austen's writing. Even as an author, Austen was reliant on help from her father and brother Henry to contact and make financial arrangements with publishers: as a woman it would have been hard to be taken seriously. Austen was actually very fortunate that her own family were supportive of her writing and could see the merit of what she had produced.

Austen's work was admired in her lifetime, even by the Prince Regent, but her greatest recognition came after her death when her books were published in a collection by Richard Bentley. Austen died in Winchester at the age of 41. Just four books were published in her lifetime, with three more later on, but her impact on the English novel is profound, paving the way from stereotypical romantic fiction to realistic and satirical studies of real life and pushing the door open further for female writers.

Right: English novelist Jane Austen, from an original family portrait

Literature, Fashion and the Arts

Aphra Behn

1640–1689 | British | Novelist and Playwright

Spy, poet, playwright, novelist and enigma: Behn's life remains partly unknown, but the essence of her genius as a writer and the force and daring of her personality have reached us through history, even when the facts of her life have largely disappeared. The first British woman known to make a living from writing and famous in her own time, she succeeded by any means.

The details of Behn's birth are not certain, but according to several reports her parents were a barber and a wet nurse living in Kent. Her name at birth was thought to be Eaffrey Johnson. Growing up against the backdrop of the English Civil War, she was a royalist who supported the Stuart line. In around 1663 she visited Surinam, an English colony, where she stayed on a plantation and saw slaves at work. Her impressions of slavery formed some of the basis for her most famous work, *Oroonoko*: the story of a royal slave. She was referred to in Surinam as Astrea, a name which was later to be her pen name and her code name as a spy; a possible indication that her spying career had already begun.

She married John Behn, a merchant, in 1664 and although he died shortly afterwards, Behn kept his name. On her return from Surinam she worked for Charles II as a spy in Antwerp in the second Anglo-Dutch War, where her role was probably as a honey-trap to turn Dutch spies into double agents. In spite of her efforts, Charles was a poor payer and Behn was left penniless on her return. There is speculation that she spent time in debtors' prison, but by 1669 she had begun to make her living by writing plays.

In the 1670s, the theatre was literally born out of politics. No playwriting and few performances had taken place in the brief Republic led by Cromwell, but when Charles II returned to England in 1660 he immediately gave permission for two new theatres: the King's Company and the Duke's Company. Many of the plays written at this time also show some of the political turbulence of the time and Behn's are no exception; working for the Duke's Company, she used her plays, which were in some cases bawdy, to mock the King's enemies and any who seemed likely to obstruct Charles's brother from inheriting the throne.

Restoration theatre was also the first time that women were allowed to act on stage in England (their parts before had been taken by young boys,) and Behn used this to her advantage, using star actress Elizabeth Barry as an instrument for her work by writing parts for her, such as the courtesan in *The Revenge*, which revealed the complex roles of marginal women in society: prostitutes and mistresses.

As the vogue for bawdy plays began to decline, Behn received more than her fair share of criticism for having written like a man. She turned her attention more towards translation, poetry and political writing but defended her rights as a writer in her preface to *The Lucky Chance*:

'If I must not, because of my Sex, have this Freedom, but that you will usurp all to your selves; I lay down my quill...'

Behn died in 1689. Her work was almost forgotten in the Victorian age, when the vogue for Christian morality made a woman writer of bawdy plays seem like an impossibility, but she was re-discovered in the 20th century.

'All women together ought to let flowers fall upon the tomb of Aphra Behn, for it was she who earned them the right to speak their minds.'

Virginia Woolf

Left: English writer and adventuress Aphra Behn became one of the first professional female authors in England

Coco Chanel

1883–1971 | French | Fashion

The name Chanel has become synonymous with style and elegance and is seen as a cornerstone of the fashion industry. The company's founder, Coco Chanel, is iconic not only within the world of fashion, but also as an early example of a highly influential businesswoman.

Gabrielle Bonheur Chanel was born illegitimately to a laundrywoman and a travelling salesman. One of five children, Gabrielle and her family moved between run-down lodgings and lived in cramped, deprived conditions. When Gabrielle's mother died at the age of 32, Gabrielle and her sister were sent to a convent for deprived and destitute girls, where they were taught to sew. When she reached the age of 18, Gabrielle was too old to stay at the convent; she left and worked as a seamstress but supplemented her income as a singer in a local café. It was here that 'Coco' (as she became known) met the first of her lovers, the wealthy Etienne Balsan. He invited her to his home in the country, where she met many rich people and led a luxurious life. One of the men she met here was to be her next lover, the even more wealthy Englishman: Arthur Capel.

Capel enabled Coco to move to Paris and helped to finance her first business in 1910, which was a milliners shop called *Chanel Modes*. Chanel hats became suddenly fashionable when a famous actress, Gabrielle Dorziat, modelled them in the play *Bel Ami*, and by 1915 Chanel was considered a 'must have' in any fashionable wardrobe. She soon became well known among the European aristocracy and befriended the Duke of Westminster and Winston Churchill.

In 1931, Chanel met Samuel Goldwyn, who invited her to Hollywood to design for films. By now, the Chanel look – simple, elegant lines in comfortable, wearable styles – were world famous. Unfortunately, however, they did not translate well onto the big screen and Chanel's designs for Hollywood movies were not considered a success, although Greta Garbo and Marlene Dietrich became private clients.

Chanel's most profitable line was her signature perfume, Chanel No. 5, but the sale of this was the cause of a bitter legal and business dispute that lasted over twenty years. Chanel licensed it as a business to Pierre Wertheimer, from whom she tried to take it back during the Second World War.

World War II provides the darkest phase in Chanel's life story. Installed in the Hotel Ritz in Paris when it was occupied by the Nazis, Chanel had a long relationship with a German officer and may have worked as a spy for the Germans. She held strongly anti-Semitic views and used the Nazis' anti-Jewish ideas to try to regain control of her perfume business from the Jewish Wertheimers, although she was ultimately unsuccessful. She also closed her factories, making 3,000 women unemployed: a move which was believed to be in part a way to avoid their demands for better pay and working conditions.

After the war, Chanel's reputation was tarnished and she moved to Switzerland. She continued to maintain a wide variety of high-society friendships and liaisons and was still actively engaged in fashion design until her death in 1971. The legacy of her work, however, has gone on and on. Chanel is credited not only as the creator of iconic perfume Chanel no. 5, but also as the designer of the original 'Little Black Dress', the Chanel suit, and many other instantly recognisable designs besides.

Top and bottom left: French designer, Coco Chanel

Bottom right: A Chanel handbag; the name is still iconic and fashionable a century later

Laurie Anderson

Born 1947 | American | Musician, Artist and Sculptor

A free, creative genius with a unique flare for originality, Anderson is a musician, artist and sculptor who has challenged the boundaries of art. Especially known for her electronic music, she is a master of blending different art forms together, with an added dash of theatrical magic.

Originally from Wayne, Illinois, Anderson graduated from Columbia University with a degree in Art History but quickly became known for her unique art forms in many different genres.

Anderson's first major work was *Automotive*, a symphony played on car horns, which Anderson first performed in 1969. Later on, in the 1970s, she produced a piece called *Duets on Ice*, in which she played a violin duet with herself whilst wearing frozen ice skates that melted as the performance went on. In 1981, her half-sung-half-spoken hit single *O Superman* was released. The song was an immediate success, reaching number two in the British singles charts and − in a break from her usual career style − she gained significant fame and recognition in the musical mainstream. It also earned her a seven-year album contract with Warner Bros. Records.

In 2003, Anderson was selected as one of NASA's first artists in residence, an event which inspired her to write *The End of the Moon*. She has continued to work on art projects in all media and film productions, while developing her career as a writer, musician, singer and artist. She married fellow musician Lou Reed in 2008.

Above: Laurie Anderson performing live at Brooklyn Academy of Music

'It's good to take a longer view and think, what would I really like to do if I had no limitations whatsoever?'

Laurie Anderson

Barbara Hepworth

1903–1975 | British | Artist

Above: Dame Barbara Hepworth with her sculpture 'Square Forms (Two Sequences)' in the grounds of the parish church of St Ives in Cornwall

One of the few women to gain international fame for her art, Barbara Hepworth is a major figure in modernist sculpture. Her curved, inviting forms are often descriptive of the relationships between two things: between the human figure and landscape, colour and texture or individual and society.

Born in Yorkshire in 1903, Hepworth studied sculpture at Leeds School of Art from 1920–1921, then the Royal College of Art from 1921–1924. After travelling extensively, however, she made her final home in St Ives in the 1930s and her home, surrounded by lovely countryside from which she drew inspiration, became a regular meeting place for artists. The town is still associated with her work today and her sculpture garden is one of its major tourist attractions. Although primarily known as a sculptor, Hepworth was also interested in presenting her sculptures in photographic form and sketched things that interested her. She took an active role in how her work was displayed in galleries.

Hepworth was married briefly in the 1920s, but her life partner was the painter Ben Nicholson, with whom she had triplets, as well as a son from her first marriage. She died at a fire in her studio when she was 72.

'I think every sculpture must be touched, it's part of the way you make it and it's really our first sensibility, it is the sense of feeling, it is first one we have when we're born. I think every person looking at a sculpture should use his own body. You can't look at a sculpture if you are going to stand stiff as a ram rod and stare at it, with as sculpture you must walk around it, bend toward it, touch it and walk away from it.'

Barbara Hepworth

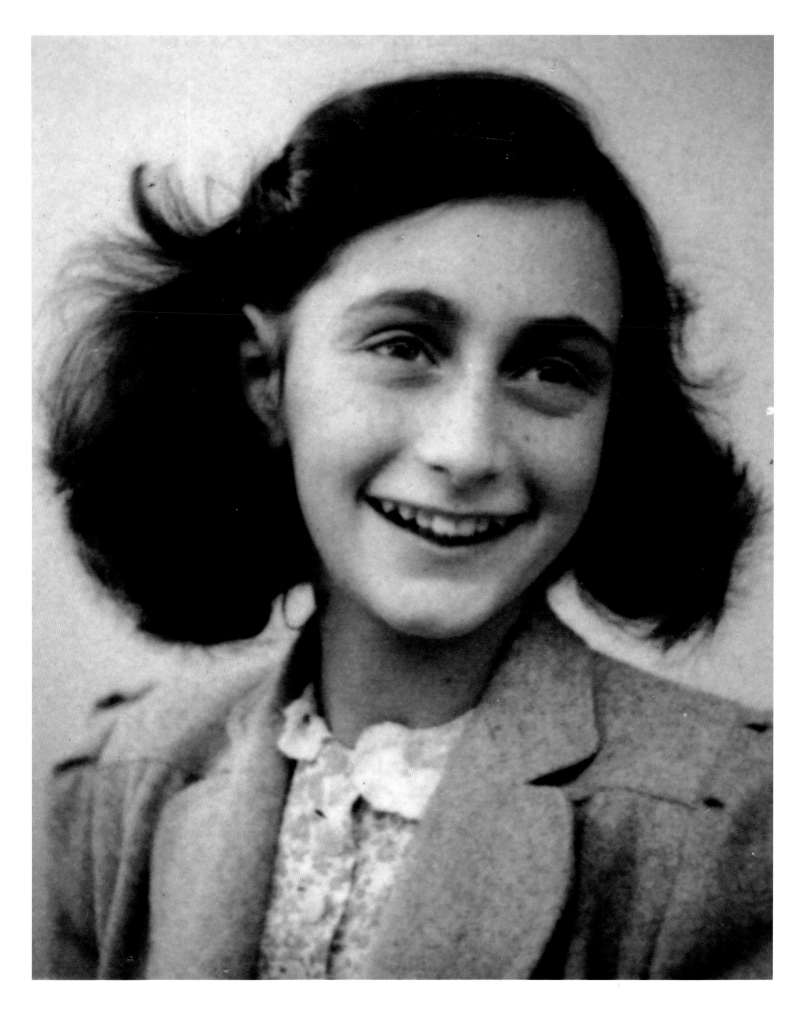

Anne Frank

1929–1945 | German | Diarist

'I want to go on living even after my death! And that's why I'm so grateful to God for having given me this gift, which I can use to develop myself and to express all that's inside me!'
Diary of Anne Frank, 5th April 1944

These prophetic words, taken from the famous diary of Anne Frank, represent the intelligence, joyfulness and hopefulness of the girl who wrote them. In spite of the tragic brevity of her life, Anne really has 'lived on' after her death.

Anne Frank was born in Frankfurt in 1929. Her parents, Otto and Edith, came from Jewish families that were successful in business, but the late 1920s and early 1930s were hard in Germany and soaring inflation made business difficult.

In 1933, Hitler became Chancellor of Germany, having risen to power with overtly anti-Semitic nationalist policies. The Franks were alarmed to see the growing change in people's attitudes towards Jewish people, who were forced out of jobs and had their businesses closed. Afraid for their future, Otto Frank moved the family to Amsterdam for good.

Once established in Amsterdam, life for the Franks returned largely to normal. Anne herself attended a Montessori kindergarten, which Otto Frank later said was good at encouraging Anne to think as an individual. It was hoped for a long time that The Netherlands would avoid any involvement in the tension that was beginning to rise around Germany.

In May 1940, however, disaster came when the Nazis invaded The Netherlands. Persecution of Jews began almost immediately. Otto Frank tried to move the family to the USA but was refused. As the situation intensified, Otto transferred ownership of his two businesses, Opekta and Pectaton, to his co-directors, rather than see them confiscated. It was these colleagues and co-workers, Victor Kugler, Johannes Kleiman, Miep Gies and Bep Voskuijl, who later concealed the Frank family in the secret annex above the Opekta offices on the Prinsengracht and who provided their link to the outside world.

The Frank family planned to go into hiding with another Jewish family, but went sooner than expected because Edith Frank received a relocation order to go to a labour camp. The family went into hiding in July 1942.

On her thirteenth birthday, just before going into hiding, Otto Frank gave Anne a book that she had admired in a shop. She used the book as a diary. As the years of confinement progressed, the book became her best friend, in which she revealed her secrets, expressed her

Left: A portrait of Anne Frank, circa 1942, from her own photo album

Literature, Fashion and the Arts

frustrations, told stories and wrote about her own ambitions. A gifted and compulsive writer, Anne described the details of her thoughts during confinement with surprising honesty and energy.

On 4th August 1944, the Franks were arrested by uniformed German police in the secret annex and taken away to prison. They were later transported to Auschwitz concentration camp. In spite of many investigations, it has never been discovered who told the Germans of their whereabouts, although in recent years it has been speculated that an investigation into ration card fraud may also have led to the raid. Once in Auschwitz, the family were separated. Anne and Margot were finally sent to Bergen-Belsen where they are believed to have died of Typhus in February 1945, just two months before the camp was liberated by the British.

The only member of the Frank family to survive was Otto. He returned to Amsterdam and to the friends who had sheltered him. One of them, Miep Gies, had preserved Anne's diary with the hope of returning it to her after the war. He gave it instead to Otto, who, on reading it, discovered not only his daughter's extraordinary gift for writing but also the dreams, ambitions and reflections she had never had the chance to tell him in real life.

Right: Anne Frank writes at her desk in Amsterdam, prior to her family going into hiding during World War II

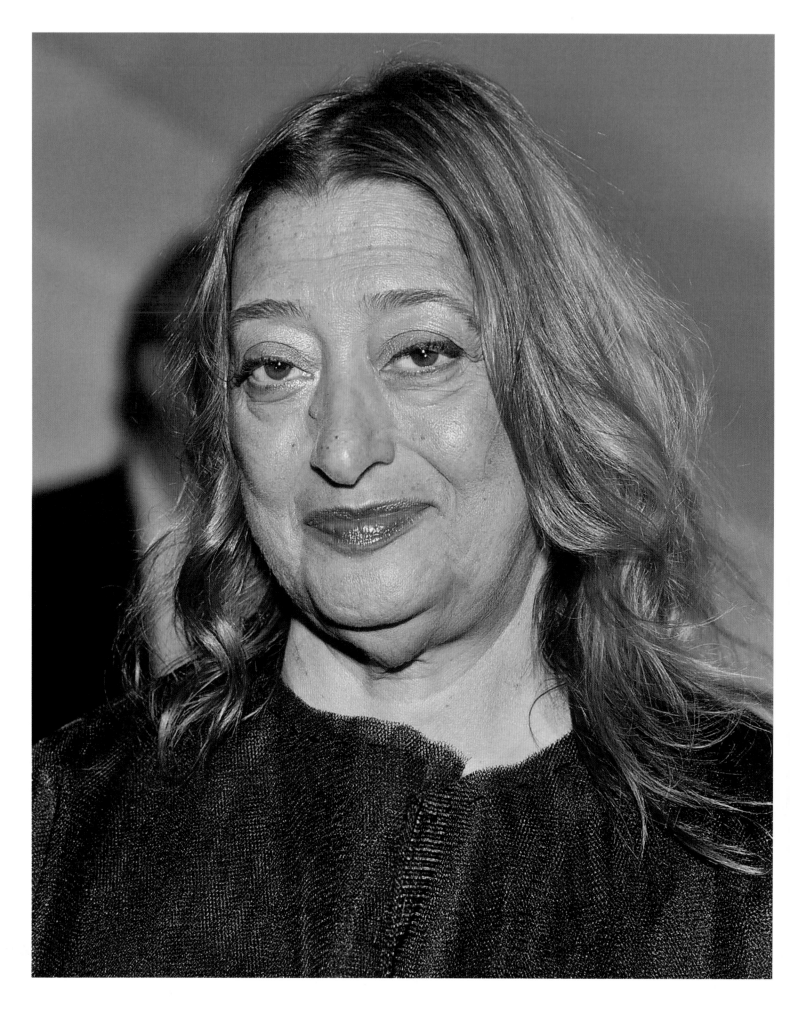

Zaha Hadid

1950–2016 | Iraqi | Architecture

Once described as 'The Queen of the curve', Hadid's striking and inviting architectural designs now grace many cities around the world. A double winner of the Stirling Prize and the first woman to win the prestigious Pritzker Architecture Prize, Hadid wrote a new chapter in building design which has brought delight to many. Her major works include the London Aquatic Centre which was used in the 2012 Olympics and the Guangzhou Opera House in China.

Hadid was born in Baghdad to a wealthy Iraqi family. Her father was an industrialist who also founded the National Democratic Party in Iraq and her mother was an artist from Mosul. Hadid spent a lot of her childhood away from Baghdad at boarding schools in Switzerland and England, so grew up with an international outlook on life. As an undergraduate, she studied maths at the American University of Beirut before moving to London to study architecture as a postgraduate. One of her lecturers, Elia Zenghelis, described her as the most outstanding pupil he had ever taught. He said, 'We called her the inventor of the 89 degrees', meaning that none of her work was based around right angles, but around fluid curves and interesting lines.

In 1980, Hadid founded her own architecture firm, Zaha Hadid Architects. Her first few years, however, met with little commercial success, although her ideas and images were admired and she had a growing reputation as an inspirational teacher and lecturer of architecture. Her first big success as an architect came in 1993, with the Vitra Fire Station for German furniture manufacturer Vitra. The building was never used as a fire station but was used as a gallery. Other striking buildings were to follow, such as the Bergisel Ski Jump in Innsbruck and the Contemporary Arts Centre in Cincinatti.

At the beginning of the 21st century, Hadid's career really began to attract international attention, with bridges such as the Zaragoza Bridge Pavilion and the Sheikh Zayed Bridge in Abu Dhabi. The long, low curve of the London Aquatics Centre, opened in 2012, epitomised the fluid lines of Hadid's design style, as did the highly unusual curving tops of the Wangjing Office Complex in Beijing.

As a naturalised British Citizen, Hadid was made a Dame of the British Empire in 2012 for her services to architecture. When she died of a heart attack in 2016 there were several projects left unfinished.

Left: Zaha Hadid at the VIP opening of The Serpentine Sackler Gallery & Autumn Exhibitions at The Serpentine Sackler Gallery, 2013

Although unusual in the world of famous architects for being an Arab woman, Hadid was not particularly keen to make a point of her nationality or gender; she wanted merely to be thought of as an architect. She was, however, keen to pass her enthusiasm and her ideas on to the next generation and enjoyed a career as a prominent professor of architecture at some of the finest educational institutions in the world. Throughout her career as an architect, Hadid lectured and held professorships at, among others, the University of Illinois, the University of Columbia and the University of Vienna, where she had the Zaha Hadid Master Class Vertical-Studio.

As a naturalised British Citizen, Hadid was made a Dame of the British Empire in 2012 for her services to architecture. When she died of a heart attack in 2016, several of her projects remained unfinished.

Following her death, Michael Kimmelman of the *New York Times* wrote of Hadid: '...her soaring structures left a mark on skylines and imaginations and in the process re-shaped architecture for the modern age...Her buildings elevated uncertainty to an art, conveyed in the odd way of one entered and moved through these buildings and in the questions that her structures raised about how they were supported...'

Right: Zaha Hadid visits the Riverside Museum, her first major public commission in the UK, in Glasgow, Scotland

Literature, Fashion and the Arts

Frida Kahlo

1907–1954 | Mexican | Artist

Frida Kahlo's striking paintings have become well known throughout the world. Her self-portraits amplify her facial features, including her trademark monobrow, with almost brutal honesty. Many of her paintings are in a naïve, colourful style which seems to rise from the heart of her native Mexico.

Born in Coyoacán in Mexico City, Kahlo was the child of a German photographer father and a Mestiza mother. Their home, La Casa Azul, is still preserved as a museum dedicated to her work. Kahlo was a bright child who, along with several of the country's future elite, went to the prestigious National Preparatory School. Rebellious and questioning as a teenager, she had a marked interest in humanitarian and justice issues. Kahlo hoped to become a doctor, but that came to an end after she was involved in a car accident at the age of 18. She had also been a childhood sufferer of polio and these two factors combined caused Kahlo ill health for most of her life.

During her long recovery from the accident, Kahlo became interested in a career as a professional artist. She also became politically engaged, joining groups that were interested in Mexican national identity, the Mexicanidad, and also the Mexican Communist Party. She met her husband, the artist Diego Rivera, through the Communist Party and the pair married in 1928.

Rivera was in receipt of a number of commissions for which he had to travel. The first was to Cuernavaca, in an area which had been affected by civil war. Here, Kahlo began to develop the naïve Mexican style for which she was to become well known. She also began to dress in a way that was more traditionally Mexican and less colonial; a style which was to become characteristic of her.

Above: Photograph of Frida Kahlo showing her recognisable hairstyle

Left: Frida Kahlo had a distinct style, both personally and in her work

Literature, Fashion and the Arts

The couple then spent three years in the US, where Rivera was honoured and the couple made a number of famous acquaintances. Kahlo was shocked by the divide between the rich and poor that she saw in the US and as a communist, did not enjoy being around capitalists like Henry Ford. However, it was here that she first displayed work of her own in exhibitions and began to consider herself an artist in her own right.

When the couple moved back to San Angel in Mexico, their marriage began to show signs of strain and Rivera began an affair with Kahlo's sister, Cristina, although they were later reconciled. The home was a hub of artistic and also communist activity, and in 1934 Leon Trotsky and his wife stayed in the house when they were exiled from Russia. Kahlo befriended and briefly had an affair with Trotsky.

Kahlo's first solo exhibition came in 1938, when she was invited to show her work in Manhattan. Her manner of dress caused a sensation in fashion-conscious New York society and her art itself was very well received. A follow-up exhibition in Paris was less successful, possibly owing to the looming threat of war, but the Louvre did buy one of her paintings, making her the first Mexican artist to achieve such an accolade.

The final years of Kahlo's life saw rising fame and declining health. She reconciled with Rivera and spent most of her time at Casa Azul taking care of the garden and painting, a quiet ending which belied the turbulence of the rest of her life.

A disabled woman from a poor country, Kahlo's work could have been easy to overlook, but her devotion to her art and her ability to unleash her unique talent has made her one of the great names in the art world and one of the leading female artists of all time.

Above: Frida Kahlo poses while painting, for a photo first published in 1931

Right: Frida had a characteristic style, typified by her self-portraits

'Nothing is absolute. Everything changes, everything moves, everything revolves, everything flies and goes away.'

Frida Kahlo

JK Rowling

Born 1965 | British | Author

Primarily known as the author of the fabulously popular *Harry Potter* novels, JK Rowling's life story is a real rags-to-riches inspiration. Since becoming famous, however, she has attracted attention for more than her writing. Her political views as well as her acts of philanthropy and connection to charity are now well documented in the press. She continues to be outspoken in many areas and to bring her influence to bear through her humanitarian views as well as by entertaining people with her stories.

Born in Gloucestershire, Rowling had a secure upbringing with her parents and younger sister, although her mother suffered with multiple sclerosis and Rowling's relationship with her father was frequently strained. Rowling went to Exeter University and then worked briefly for Amnesty International and the Chamber of Commerce before moving to Portugal to teach English. The idea for *Harry Potter* came quite early on in Rowling's working life, during her time at the Chamber of Commerce. Sitting on a delayed train, the idea for a boy going to a school for wizards arrived fully formed in her mind. Since Rowling was young and working at the time, it took several years to finish the first novel and during the time she took to write it, Rowling lost her mother, was married and then divorced, and had a child.

Her first novel, *Harry Potter and the Philosopher's Stone*, was published in 1997 and became an immediate success, although publication only came after a long struggle with publishers' rejections. Six more *Harry Potter* books followed, each of which saw the characters grow up a little and deal with the challenges of normal teenagers, as well as the battle between good and bad magic.

In October 1998, just over one year from publication, Warner Bros. bought the film rights for Harry Potter and the resulting films became some of the biggest box office successes of all time. Rowling maintained a degree of control over the casting and script for the films, revealing to the actors some things about the characters so that they would not do anything which contradicted later plot developments. For sales of books and further income from the films, Rowling has become the highest earning author of all time. The books have sold over 40 million copies.

Since finishing the *Harry Potter* series, Rowling has turned her attention to writing adult novels, particularly crime novels with a private detective protagonist called Cormoran Strike. Rowling originally had these published under a pseudonym, Robert Galbraith, so that readers and publishers would not be influenced by associations with her previous work – a different voice was needed for her new venture as a writer for adults. The connection between 'Galbraith' and Rowling was quickly uncovered, however.

Above: JK Rowling attends a preview of *Harry Potter and the Cursed Child*, a play which continues the life of the popular series of books and films

Rowling is a well known supporter of left-wing causes including the British Labour Party. She has also given significant donations to children's charities and multiple sclerosis charities. In 2006, she gave a large donation to the Centre for Regenerative Medicine at Edinburgh University which is now named after her mother, Anne Rowling. She is also a prominent figure with the Gingerbread, a charity that supports single parents.

Right, top: Rowling illuminates the Empire State Building to mark the USA launch of her non-profit children's organisation, Lumos

Right, below: Daniel Radcliffe, JK Rowling, Emma Watson and Rupert Grint attend the *Harry Potter And The Deathly Hallows Part 2* world premiere

CHAPTER 3:
Activists and Revolutionaries

Activists and Revolutionaries

The Suffragettes

Late 19th Century | British and American | Women's Rights

We take our involvement in politics for granted now, but for most of history women have not had the right to vote in elections. As women's lives were mainly conducted at home or only in menial jobs, their voices were rarely heard in public. This meant that it was a surprise to some people when, in the 19th century, women started to protest about their inability to air their political views. Women who took part in the organisation to demand female 'suffrage', as voting is sometimes called, were called The Suffragettes.

Women finally 'won' the right to vote in 1918. This was partly as a result of their campaigning and partly owing to the enhanced role played by women at work during World War I. Here are some of the women who led the movement for suffrage.

Emmeline Pankhurst (1858–1928)

One of the main organisers of the campaign for female suffrage was Emmeline Pankhurst. Born in 1958, she founded the Women's Social and Political Union in 1903, which became a focal point for the campaign. It was her decision to use 'direct action' as a campaign style: this meant that they drew attention to their cause with acts of disruption and sabotage in order to publicise their cause. They never hurt people, but they damaged property and wrote their slogan 'Votes for women' on public buildings. They did this because they knew that the cause needed publicity. When the women were arrested for minor acts of vandalism like smashing windows or public disorder, they were then able to talk about female suffrage in court and get it reported in the newspapers. By doing this they brought their views to a new audience. They also went on hunger-strike in prison to make their imprisonment more newsworthy.

When women over the age of 30 were given the vote in 1918, Pankhurst joined the Conservative Party in order to start a new campaign for child welfare. By the time she died in 1928, all women over 21 were allowed to vote.

Left: English feminist suffrage leader Emmeline Pankhurst, who led the movement to win the vote for women in Great Britain

Below: Emmeline Pankhurst with fellow suffragettes and a noticeable police presence

Activists and Revolutionaries

Emily Davison (1872–1913)

In 1913, Emily Davison became legendary when she carried out one of the most famous and fatal acts of the suffrage campaign. Amidst crowds that had gathered to watch the Derby – a famous horse race – Emily squeezed under the rail and threw herself under the King's horse. She died a few days later from her injuries, but it was not her only act of self sacrifice. She had already been imprisoned for acts of vandalism and had been violently force-fed with a tube in her nose when she had refused food in prison.

Below: A march of an estimated 50,000 women, despite rainy conditions, is led by Emmeline Pankhurst

Right: Pankhurst if arrested outside of Buckingham Palace, while trying to deliver a petition to HM King George V, May 1914

Susan B Anthony (1820–1906)

Born on 15th February 1820, in Massachusetts USA, Anthony worked as a teacher before becoming a leading figure in the anti-slavery and women's voting rights movement. She partnered with Elizabeth Cady Stanton and led the National American Woman Suffrage Association in 1869. Anthony died on 13th March 1906, 14 years before women were finally given the vote.

Elizabeth Cady Stanton (1815–1902)

Born in Johnstown, New York, Stanton was an active anti-slavery campaigner with her husband, Henry Brewster Stanton (co-founder of the Republican Party), and campaigner for women's rights. Unlike many of those involved in the women's rights movement, Stanton addressed various issues affecting women beyond suffrage. Her concerns included maternity rights, property, and the right to birth control.

Mother Teresa (Anjezë Gonxhe Bojaxhiu)

1910–1977 | Macedonian | Missionary and Nobel Winner

Mother Teresa became famous around the world as the human epitome of kindness, compassion and self-sacrifice for her work in the slums of Calcutta. Her worn face and diminutive figure seemed to be most at home amongst the throng of desperate people who needed her most. It is this selfless dedication to helping others for which, after her death, she was eventually canonised and is now known as Saint Teresa.

Anjezë (or Agnes) Gonxhe Bojaxhiu, as Mother Teresa was known at birth, was born in Skopje, Macedonia on 26th August 1910. Of Albanian descent, she felt the call of the Church after being inspired by stories of missionaries and their works, and from the age of 12 knew that she wanted to join the Catholic Church as a nun.

At 18 she left home to join an Irish community of nuns known as the Sisters of Loreto and never saw her family again. In preparation for her calling, she was sent to Loreto Abbey near Dublin where she also learned to speak English, the language of the mission. Agnes arrived as a novitiate at her first posting at Darjeeling in 1929, and two years later she made her first vows and took the name Teresa, after St Teresa of Lisieux, the patron saint of missionaries. After moving to Calcutta she taught at St Mary's High School and there, on 14th May 1927, Teresa took her final vows.

Outside the school where Teresa taught lay the heaving slums full of illiterate, desperately poor and completely overlooked people. Their plight worsened after the famine of 1943 and the sectarian violence during Indian Partition in 1946. Mother Teresa felt compelled to help these people, and in 1948 she at last received permission to leave the school and devote herself to the people of the slums. She also took Indian citizenship.

Although lacking any funding, Mother Teresa set up an open-air school in Motijhil for the children of the slums, but she had to beg for supplies and food. However, as her work became known, she was joined by volunteer helpers and aided by financial contributions.

Above: Mother Teresa and the poor in Calcutta, India in October, 1979

Left: Princess Diana, Princess of Wales holds hands with Mother Teresa following a meeting in the Bronx on June 18, 1997 in New York

Activists and Revolutionaries

In 1950, Pope Pius XII granted Mother Teresa permission to start her own religious order with 13 members in Calcutta. In time this led to the creation of the Missionaries of Charity. By the 1960s, the order had orphanages, hospices and leper shelters across India, and within a decade Mother Teresa had become an international celebrity.

The order became an International Religious Family with active and contemplative branches around the world. In 1979 Mother Teresa won the Nobel Peace Prize for her work with the poor, orphaned, sick and dying.

It was in 1983 that Mother Teresa suffered her first heart attack, continuing to suffer from heart troubles for the remainder of her life. She died of another heart attack on 5th September 1997. By the time she died, the Missionaries of Charity were operating 610 missions in 123 countries.

Right: Mother Teresa prays at the ruins of a Church

Below: Mother Teresa accompanied by children at her mission in Calcutta

Jeanne D'Arc (Joan of Arc)

1412–1431 | French | Revolutionary and Saint

By the age of 19, Joan of Arc had led an army into battle, been captured, tried and killed. Centuries after her martyrdom, in 1909, she was made a Roman Catholic Saint in recognition of her devout nature and her patriotism. A symbol of French nationhood and Christian devotion, Joan of Arc's remarkable and tragic story has inspired generations of artists, storytellers and musicians.

In 1415, the English invaded France with the ambition of taking France under English rule. Several years of confusion followed where rival groups wanted their own candidate for King. The Burgundians, who supported the English, favoured the son of the English Henry V. The French 'Armagnac faction' supported the son of King Charles VI, who was to become Charles VII.

Meanwhile, born in 1412, Joan was living a quiet life growing up in Domrémy with her parents. Her mother was a devout Christian who encouraged her daughter to share her beliefs. By the time Joan was a teenager, she began to see religious visions in which Saint Michael and Saint Catherine urged her to visit the Dauphin (Charles VII) and ask him to let her expel the English so that he could ascend the throne unchallenged.

As a young female peasant, accessing the ear of the Dauphin should have been impossible, but Joan petitioned the garrison commander at a town near to her home, Vaucouleurs, to take her to see him. The garrison commander was initially sceptical, but after Joan predicted a change in the army's fortunes at the Battle of Rouvray near Orleans, he began to take her at her word and escorted her to the Dauphin. Joan started to wear men's clothes as a precaution, as she had to travel through Burgundian-held areas and did not want to draw attention to herself. When shown in art, she is often dressed as a man.

Above: French heroine and Catholic Saint, St Jeanne is often shown wearing male clothing or armour

Left: A 19th century chromolithograph depicting Joan of Arc as she is burnt at stake in the market place at Rouen, following her trial for heresy and sorcery

Activists and Revolutionaries

Joan met the Dauphin in 1429 when she was just 17. She asked if she could lead the army into its next battle at Orleans, claiming that she alone would be able to lift the siege there. The English had been trying to take the city of Orleans since 1428, as it was of considerable strategic importance. Many felt that if Orleans fell to the English they would win the whole of France. Amazingly, Charles agreed to Joan's request with the backing of his courtiers.

At Orleans, Joan arrived on 29th April. She gave advice to the commanders and stood in the battle with her banner. By 8th May the siege was over and the English were in retreat. More victories followed as Joan urged a march on Reims so that the Dauphin could be crowned Charles VII.

The coronation of Charles VII took place at Reims Cathedral on 17th July. The French believed that, through Joan, God was on their side. The English, meanwhile, saw her as an agent of the devil.

Following this swift round of victories, Charles' court sought to make peace but were tricked by the Burgundians. Some close-fought battles took place around Paris with both sides scoring victories as well as suffering defeats. In a skirmish near Compiegne, Joan was finally ambushed and imprisoned by the English. She was tried on made-up counts of heresy in an attempt to embarrass Charles. She performed well at her trial, but was tricked into signing a confession on pain of death. On 30th May 1431, Joan was burned at the stake and her ashes were thrown into the river Seine.

Below: An engraving showing Joan entering Orleans

Right: Jean Seberg plays the title role of the 1957 film, *Saint Joan*

Masoumeh Ebtekar

Born 1960 | Iranian | Activist, Scientist and Politician

Activist, scientist, politician, author and campaigner for women, Ebtekar has had a varied, influential and somewhat surprising life in the public eye ever since the age of 19. Although some of her actions have attracted controversy, her success and ambition continue to provide a focal point for women in the Islamic world and everywhere.

Born into a wealthy and well-educated family, Ebtekar was initially known as Niloufar. Her father studied in Philadelphia for six years, leaving Ebtekar with an excellent command of English throughout her life. On returning to Tehran, Ebtekar studied at the International School.

Ebtekar first became well known internationally as the spokesperson for a group of students who, in 1979, captured the US embassy in Tehran and took hostages in protest of the USA's failure to support the Iranian Revolution. It became one of the longest-running hostage situations in history, lasting for 444 days. Because of her good command of English, Ebtekar, known at the time of the crisis by the pseudonym 'Mary', was the spokesperson and translator between the students and the USA.

Continuing her studies after the hostage crisis, Ebtekar became a noted academic in the field of immunology, gaining her MSc and PhD at Tarbiat Modares University in Tehran. She still lectures there and supervises postgraduate students, and works as a reviewer on several international immunology journals. She has also published a number of her own articles on immunology.

In 1997, Ebtekar took up her first role in government under President Khatami. She was made head of the Department for the Environment, where she undertook several important structural and organisational changes. In the early years of the 20th century she also took part in a number of international conferences discussing environmental issues and in May 2005 chaired a significant environmental conference in Tehran, organised by the UN.

Ebtekar also became involved in speaking out over women's issues, criticising the Taliban for their treatment of women in Afghanistan and representing the network of women's NGOs (non-government organisations) in Tehran. In 2009 she considered running for the Presidency of Iran, but pulled out before the election, perhaps fearing that the country was not yet ready for a female President.

In 2013, Ebtekar took up the same position again as head of environmental affairs under President Rouhani and began a series of major improvements to the environment, including the national Low Carbon Energy strategy. In 2017, she was given a new appointment as Head of Women's Affairs.

Above: Masoumeh Ebtekar, vice-president of the Islamic Republic of Iran in a discussion during the World Economic Forum in Davos, Switzerland

Ebtekar has written books about political events in her life, including one about her time as 'Mary', the spokesperson for the Iranian hostage takers. In this autobiographical work, *Takeover in Tehran: The Inside Story of the 1979 U.S. Embassy Capture*, she explains her reasons for supporting the students, and for her antagonism towards the US at the time. Her reputation in the USA remains controversial. She has also written extensively about the particular role of women working for peace and improvements to the global environment. In her essay entitled 'Peace and Sustainability Depend on the Spiritual and the Feminine', Ebtekar provides her views on the interrelated nature of peace and sustainable development. In 2006, Ebtekar was named as a Champion of the Earth by the United Nations Environment Programme for her continued efforts, as part of her government, to bring about environmental change in Iran and the wider world.

In a dizzyingly busy and far-reaching professional life, Ebtekar continues to represent her political, environmental and religious views with unflinching honesty, driving progress in all areas as she goes.

Above: French Foreign Minister Laurent Fabius and Masoumeh Ebtekar,
hold a press conference following their meeting in Tehran, Iran, in July 2015

Betty Friedan

1921–2006 | American | Activist, Feminist and Author

Born in the 1920s, Friedan, (born Betty Naomi Goldstein,) could have lived the life pre-ordained for the majority of women in her generation: a limited choice of jobs; marriage; motherhood. Instead, she sought to understand and expose the real feelings of women about their unliberated existences. She further sought to expose the potential of all women to work outside the home and take a fuller role in society.

In her book, *The Female Mystique*, Friedan described the attitude of women to their own lives as 'The problem that has no name':

The problem lay buried, unspoken, for many years in the minds of American women. It was a strange stirring, a sense of dissatisfaction, a yearning [that is, a longing] that women suffered in the middle of the 20th century in the United States. Each suburban [house]wife struggled with it alone. As she made the beds, shopped for groceries ... she was afraid to ask even of herself the silent question — 'Is this all?'

Friedan started her research for the book by conducting a survey of the feelings of her fellow graduates and found that many felt the same. They wanted intellectual stimulation and recognition, not just the life of a homemaker. Friedan's inspiration for this research came from her own life. After graduating from Berkeley, she pursued a career as a journalist working for left-leaning publications, during which time she married and had her first child. When pregnant with her second child, however, she was fired from her job and found herself at home as a full-time mother. She felt isolated, alone and terrified. Finding that other women felt the same, she went on to make her first publication, which quickly became a best-seller.

Although a supporter of women's rights, Friedan did not agree with some extreme feminists who were antagonistic towards both men and women who chose to be homemakers. Friedan's idea was to promote the idea of choice.

In 1966, Friedan co-founded the National Organization for Women (NOW). The organisation was established in order to enforce the laws surrounding equal rights for women on pay and employment. A key moment for women's rights came in 1970, when Friedan organised the national Women's Strike for Equality and led a march of an estimated 20,000 women in New York City. While the march's primary objective was promoting equal opportunities for women in jobs and education, protesters and organisers of the event also protested about abortion rights and the establishment of childcare centres.

Left: American writer and feminist Betty Friedan at her apartment in New York City, 1990

Activists and Revolutionaries

Married once to Carl Friedan, Betty Friedan's marriage ended in divorce in 1969. Although the couple had three children, the marriage was reported to be stormy and violent at times. Betty Friedan could be a demanding and selfish individual, although many around her considered these qualities to have been essential qualities for driving change in the way that she did.

In an article in The Guardian, 2006, Germaine Greer said this:

Betty Friedan 'changed the course of human history almost single-handedly.' Her ex-husband, Carl Friedan, believes this; Betty believed it too. This belief was the key to a good deal of Betty's behaviour; she would become breathless with outrage if she didn't get the deference she thought she deserved. Though her behaviour was often tiresome, I figured that she had a point. Women don't get the respect they deserve unless they are wielding male-shaped power; if they represent women they will be called 'love' and expected to clear up after themselves. Betty wanted to change that for ever.

Right: Betty Friedan at a party for President Jimmy Carter, Long Island, New York, 1976

Above: Dr Kathryn F Clarenbach (left) of the University of Wisconsin as chairman of the board and author Betty Friedan of New York (right) as president The National Organization for Women (NOW), 1968

Helen Keller

1880–1968 | American | Civil Rights and Suffragette

If Keller's life tells us one thing, it is that she refused to be defined by her disability. She wanted to show that she could think, believe and try anything that she wanted.

At the time Helen Keller was born, a disabled person was considered a burden to the family as they could make no contribution. Education and medical opportunities to improve the outlook of a disabled person were scarce. Keller spent her life proving that, with the right education and opportunities, disabled people could bring as much to society as able-bodied people.

Born with sight and hearing, Keller contracted a serious illness at the age of 19 months that left her blind and deaf. At first, Keller was so frustrated that she resorted to tantrums, but she did establish a basic system of signage with the daughter of the cook who lived with them. Keller's mother, however, was inspired by Charles Dickens' *American Notes* about a deaf and blind girl called Laura Bridgman and set out to find a way of communicating with her daughter. After several inquiries, Keller and her father arrived at the Perkins Institute for the Blind in South Boston. Here, they were placed in the care of Anne Sullivan, a 20-year-old graduate of the school, who believed she could teach Helen to read and sign.

Above: Cancelled stamp from the US featuring Helen Keller and her teacher, Anne Sullivan

Right: Photograph of Helen Keller, circa 1950

'Until the great mass of the people shall be filled with the sense of responsibility for each other's welfare, social justice can never be attained.'

Helen Keller

Activists and Revolutionaries

Over the next few years, Sullivan taught Keller through various methods: Braille, finger signing and touch-lip reading. Keller became so proficient that she was able to go to school and then to Radcliffe College, where she became the first deaf-blind person ever to obtain a Bachelor's degree. She also met many famous people including writer Mark Twain, with whom she became friends.

Following graduation, Keller wrote several books about her life which shed new light on the life of someone who was deaf and blind, including *The Story of My Life* and *The World I Live In*. She became an advocate for the deaf and blind and significantly raised recognition of the issues faced by those living with these disabilities. Although unable to hear the sound of her own voice, she learned to speak and eventually visited 25 countries to talk about disability issues.

In her 20s, Keller also became involved with socialism, civil rights and the suffragette cause. She was a founding member of the American Civil Liberties Union. Her socialist views, however, were not without their critics, as many in the USA were worried about the rise of socialism. Keller claimed that many who praised her when she talked about her disabilities only began to emphasise her disabilities when she talked about socialism. Eventually, some of her writings were banned in the press, as she was considered a radical.

This, however, did not prevent her from her activism and she remained a socialist throughout her life. She was particularly articulate about the lack of responsibility that rich capitalists took over their workers: many disabilities including blindness, deafness and physical impairments were caused by working conditions, and the cause of poverty.

Right: Headshot portrait of American educator and activist for the disabled, Helen Keller, 1956. A childhood illness left Keller deaf, mute, and blind

Rosa Parks

1913–2005 | American | Civil Rights Protester

Perhaps it is the mundane beginning of Rosa Parks's great stand against oppression that makes it all the more remarkable. That a tired woman's refusal to vacate her seat on a bus should cause her to be arrested and tried, perhaps brought to light the ridiculous and unnatural nature of segregation. Parks' refusal to back down throughout the arrest and trial process, her courage in the face of habitual and routine oppression and her example to the civil rights movement were to prove pivotal factors in the advancement of equality in the USA.

In the first half of the 20th century, black and white people were segregated in virtually every aspect of daily life in the southern United States by the 'Jim Crow' laws. Train and bus companies were not required to provide separate vehicles for the different races, but they did adopt a seating policy that established separate sections for blacks and whites. School bus transportation was unavailable in any form for black school children in the South.

Rosa Parks remembered attending elementary school in Pine Level, where school buses took white students to their new school and black students had to walk to theirs:

 'I'd see the bus pass every day ... But to me, that was a way of life; we had no choice but to accept what was the custom. The bus was among the first ways I realized there was a black world and a white world.'

Rosa Louise McCauley was born in Tuskegee, Alabama in 1913. In her adult life she would later move to Montgomery, Alabama where she married Raymond Parks, took a job as a seamstress at the Montgomery Fair department store and became involved with the local branch of the National Association for the Advancement of Colored People (NAACP).

On 1st December 1955, Parks was riding the Cleveland Avenue bus, sitting in the appropriate 'colored section,' when the bus driver, James Blake, asked Parks and three others to vacate their seats in order to make room for white passengers who were boarding. Three of those people complied with Blake's request but Parks refused. Blake called the police and had Parks arrested. This simple act of civil disobedience by the 42-year-old Parks, a woman simply trying to get home after a day's work, galvanised the local black community and spearheaded the Montgomery Bus Boycott.

Tried and convicted of disorderly conduct and violating a local segregation ordinance, Parks later appealed her conviction and challenged the legality of racial segregation.

In 1992, Parks told Lynn Neary of National Public Radio, *'I did not want to be mistreated, I did not want to be deprived of a seat that I had paid for. It was just time ... there was opportunity for me to take a stand to express the way I felt about being treated in that manner'.*

Right: Portrait of Rosa Parks, who organized the boycott of buses in Montgomery, Alabama, 1955

Above: Rosa Parks displays her Congressional Gold Medal of Honor with US Vice President Al Gore, prior to a benefit tribute concert in her honour, 1999 in Detroit

Activists and Revolutionaries

Her defiance raised the profile of the civil rights movement
and Parks went on to work with Martin Luther King, helping
him to acquire national prominence for their campaign.
Time Magazine voted Rosa Parks one of the 100 Most
Influential People of the 20th Century. She was awarded
the Medal of Freedom, the highest award given to a civilian
citizen, by President Bill Clinton in 1996.

When she died in 2005, Rosa was the first woman to lie in
honour in the US Capitol rotunda, where her casket was
visited by over 50,000 people and her funeral was nationally
televised. She is widely heralded as the 'Mother of the Civil
Rights Movement'.

Right: Rosa Parks, pictured in the centre, rides on a newly integrated bus following the Supreme Court ruling, ending a successful 381 day boycott of segregated buses

Margaret Sanger

1879–1966 | American | Birth Control Campaigner

In trying to name the biggest revolution in women's everyday lives in the last century, it is difficult to look beyond birth control, as it is from the development of birth control that so many other changes in women's lives have come. Most women now cannot imagine the lives that their female ancestors led, in a constant battle against their own bodies; struggling with repeated pregnancy both wanted and unwanted. In the early part of the 20th century, some women began a protest against the religious and social norms of the day to give women control over their own fertility. In doing so, they risked scandal and even imprisonment. One of the foremost women in this struggle was US-born Margaret Sanger.

A trained nurse, Sanger saw at first hand, all too often, the awfulness of women's lives when they were forced into illegal abortions, too-frequent pregnancies and lives with children that they hadn't the money to feed, let alone bring up. Sanger's own mother, born in Ireland, had 18 pregnancies of which only 11 were successful and died young, so Sanger knew the potential misery of uncontrolled fertility from her own life.

Born Margaret Higgins, Sanger was the daughter of a free-thinking stonemason who became an atheist and who was also an activist for the causes of female suffrage and public education. Her mother held more orthodox Catholic views. Sanger herself initially seemed destined to lead an unremarkable life as a nurse, wife and mother. She married architect William Sanger and gave up her education to start a family. In 1911, however, the couple's house was destroyed by fire and they moved to New York City, where Sanger went to work as a nurse. While working amongst the city's poorer citizens, she became acutely aware of the problems caused by uncontrolled, repeated pregnancies and began campaigning for improvements to women's rights.

Sanger also became involved in the New York political scene. In 1912, she started writing a newspaper column called 'What Every Girl Should Know' to educate women and girls about how to prevent conception. The column was highly controversial but led, in 1914, to a monthly magazine called *The Woman Rebel*, which promoted a woman's right to birth control. Unfortunately, the publication of this magazine led her into trouble under the Comstock Act, a law passed in 1873 which made it illegal to promote 'obscene and immoral materials'. Rather than face prosecution, Sanger fled to England until the charges were dropped. Whilst in England, she met other birth control activists and progressive thinkers, including Marie Stopes and HG Wells.

On returning to the US, Sanger opened the first birth-control clinic in Brooklyn. The clinic was raided after nine days, again under the Comstock Act, and Sanger was arrested, but under appeal the law was altered so that contraception could be recommended by doctors. A legal birth control clinic followed in 1923 and Sanger continued to campaign for better information for women and better contraceptive facilities through the National Committee on Federal Legislation for Birth Control.

Some of Sanger's views attracted controversy. She was to some extent a supporter of eugenics, or selective breeding, as she felt that some people were incapable of 'responsible' parenting. She has also been accused of racism, although in reality she rejected racist notions and was concerned with helping African American women become more aware of their choices.

What seems beyond question is that Sanger's actions were grounded in compassion for women.

'No woman can call herself free who does not own and control her body. No woman can call herself free until she can choose consciously whether she will or will not be a mother.'

Margaret Sanger

Right: A portrait from the 1920s of Margaret Sanger taken in her clinic in Brooklyn, New York, the day it was to be closed down by authorities. She was the founder of the first North American family planning centre

Diana Spencer (Princess of Wales)

1961–1997 | British | Humanitarian and AIDS Campaigner

Princess Diana was one of the most recognisable figures of the late 20th century. Popular and charming, she introduced a new phase in the history of the British royal family because of her informality and approachability. Although she was capable of jealousy and moodiness, she wasn't afraid to show her true nature: something the royal family has striven hard to avoid for centuries. Her impact on the royal family, and the world, was profound.

Born Lady Diana Frances Spencer, Diana's aristocratic family was always well known in royal circles and her ancestral home was at Althorp House in Northamptonshire. Diana was educated first at Riddlesworth Hall and then at a finishing school in Switzerland. Returning to England, she took up a job as a kindergarten teacher in London.

In 1980, Diana's life changed forever when she was linked with Charles, Prince of Wales: the eldest son of Queen Elizabeth II and heir to the throne. Charles had been a bachelor until he was in his thirties, although he had been in romantic relationships and there was speculation about which eligible lady would be his final choice of bride.

Diana became engaged to Charles and in a foretaste of what was to come, she was hounded by the tabloid press. The couple met surprisingly few times before the wedding and some expressed surprise at the difference in their ages.

The wedding took place in St Paul's Cathedral in 1981 and in her vows, Diana famously got the groom's name wrong. The nation, however, celebrated. The wedding was watched on television by millions of people, and thousands came out into the streets of London and waved flags as the couple's coach drove along.

Left: Diana, Princess of Wales, at Neves Bendinha, an ICRC Orthopaedic Workshop in Luanda, Angola

Above: Princess Diana carries Prince Henry (Harry) on her shoulders at Highgrove, 1986

Activists and Revolutionaries

Diana now took on her public role as a member of the royal family. She gave birth to her first child and the second in line to the throne, William Arthur Philip Louis, in 1982. A second son, Henry Charles Albert David, to be known as 'Harry', was born in 1984. Diana's natural warmth and ability to relate to people from every walk of life made her extremely popular with the British public, but her relationship with Prince Charles became more and more strained in the late 1980s. The pair finally separated in 1992 amidst scandals, in which each of the pair were rumoured to be seeing other people. A full divorce was granted in 1996.

The princess did not retire from public life, however, but took on an increasing number of charitable and humanitarian roles. She worked with AIDS charities and played a prominent role in the campaign to clear abandoned landmines in war-torn countries. As the press continued to run stories about her private life, Diana embarked on public interviews to give her side of the events surrounding her marriage to Prince Charles.

In 1997, Diana also appeared to have found personal happiness in her relationship with Dodi Fayed, the son of the owner of the prestigious Harrods store in central London, until both were suddenly and shockingly killed in a car crash in a Paris underpass in 1997. The most likely cause of the crash was excessive speed by their driver as he attempted to escape a pack of relentless tabloid photographers. Neither Diana nor Dodi was wearing a seatbelt.

In his funeral address, Diana's brother described her as 'the most hunted person of the modern age': an irony, since the Goddess Diana is herself 'the hunter'. Diana's passing led to an unparalleled wave of national mourning and her funeral was watched by tens of millions.

Perhaps Diana's greatest legacy to the world is her two sons. Aged just 16 and 13 when she died, they have grown up to share many of their mother's values and have blazed a trail in compassionate and humanitarian activities.

Above: The Princess of Wales touching members of the untouchable class during a visit to Hyderabad, India, February 1992

Right: A portrait of Diana, Princess of Wales, circa 1995

Harriet Tubman

1821–1913 | American | Anti-Slavery Campaigner

Undoubtedly one of the darkest passages in American history, slavery was still commonplace in the 19th Century in the southern states of the US until the end of the Civil War in 1865. Harriet Tubman, an African American, was born into slavery but she was a passionate believer in the right of African Americans to be free, convinced it was the will of God. She not only escaped her own slavery but helped hundreds of others to freedom as well.

Tubman was born in Maryland as a slave. Her precise birthdate is unknown but is believed to be between 1820 and 1822. Her parents were both slaves; her mother was a cook in a large house and her father was a forester. Harriet worked from an early age. She was beaten and at one time received a head injury so serious it left her with a form of epilepsy throughout her life.

In the 1840s, Tubman's owner died, leading to fears that her family would be sold separately and split up. To Tubman, this was unacceptable. Making arrangements, she escaped in 1849 and was taken from hiding place to hiding place along the 'Underground Railroad', a secret sequence of safe houses held by people who were against slavery. Tubman had to travel by night, sometimes hidden in carts, until she finally reached the state of Pennsylvania, where she was, by rights, a free woman.

Tubman, however, was not content to be free while her family were still slaves. Earning a little money from menial jobs, she maintained her contact with those on the 'Underground Railroad' and became a 'conductor', rescuing her own family members as well as many others. She made around 13 trips in all and in one of her final visits

to Dorchester County, where she had been a slave, rescued her own parents and led them to safety.

In 1861, at the outbreak of the Civil War, Tubman made herself useful as a nurse on the side of the Union, believing that a victory by the Unionists over the Confederates was more likely to lead to the end of slavery. When Abraham Lincoln made the Declaration of Emancipation, the effective legal end to slavery, she redoubled her efforts and became a scout within the army, finding essential intelligence and passing it to the Union commanders. She famously became the first woman to lead an armed assault, using her specialised knowledge to capture plantations on the Combahee river, freeing more than 700 slaves. She then spent two more years caring for slaves and soldiers alike.

After the war, Tubman returned to the home she had been allowed to buy from a supporter in Auburn, which was where several of her family including her parents stayed. Tubman married an ex-soldier from one of the coloured divisions and although he was much younger than her, the two lived happily and adopted a daughter.

She became a speaker for female suffrage in her later years, but her selfless campaigning often left her penniless, even while she was famous. She was eventually granted a war pension for her work as a nurse in 1898.

Tubman died in 1913. Already well known, in death her memory became a guiding light not only for African Americans or for women, but for the true, eclectic heart of America.

'When I found I had crossed that line, I looked at my hands to see if I was the same person. There was such a glory over everything; the sun came like gold through the trees, and over the fields, and I felt like I was in Heaven.'

Harriet Tubman

Right: A portrait of Harriet Tubman, African-American abolitionist and Union spy during the American Civil War, circa 1870

Malala Yousafzai

Born 1997 | Pakistan | Blogger and Activist

On 9th October 2012, Malala Yousafzai's world was changed forever when a man with a gun boarded a bus that she was sitting on, as she travelled home from school. He asked for her by name and when she answered, he shot her in the head. Yousafzai was just 15 at the time. In spite of her young age, the shooting was no accident: it was a carefully targeted operation and Yousafzai had been threatened for months before it happened. A blogger, activist and documentary subject, Yousafzai had been an outspoken opponent of the Taliban and a supporter of women's rights in her native Mingora, in the Swat District of Pakistan.

Born in 1997, Yousafzai was brought up in a reforming home: her father was a Pakistani humanitarian and activist with progressive views on women's lives and education. He ran several schools and his views on education had a profound impact on his daughter, whom he encouraged to be a politician when she grew up. Taking Benazir Bhutto as a role model, Yousafzai first became a secret blogger for BBC Urdu, writing about her life growing up in an area which was contested between the Taliban and the Pakistani military. In the Swat Valley where she lived, the ultra-conservative Muslim Taliban had begun burning schools and forbidding girls and women to be seen outside. These were not the views of the central Pakistani government and the rule of the area was fought over by the two sides.

Yousafzai came to be well known in Pakistan as a child activist against the Taliban. In 2009, while displaced from her home in Swat because of the fighting between the Taliban and the military, she was interviewed on AVT-Khyber about her political views. She was also the subject of a US documentary. Although her identity as the blogger for BBC Urdu had been concealed, it became known who she was and she and her father became the subject of threats. She was, however, honoured by many. She was nominated by Desmond Tutu for the Children's International Peace Prize and was awarded Pakistan's National Youth Peace Prize.

On her return to Swat, Yousafzai continued her education, although the Taliban were still active in the area and many were afraid to take part in any actions that might bring reprisals. Girls stayed away from school and those that did go wore plain clothes as a disguise.

Yousafzai's shooting in 2012 caused national and international outrage. Her attackers were immediately hunted down and Yousafzai was offered medical help from all over the world. After initially receiving treatment for her head wound in Pakistan, Yousafzai was flown to Birmingham for continued treatment, where a titanium plate was fitted to her skull and she was given a cochlea implant.

Since recovering, Yousafzai has become an important figure in world politics. Wise beyond her years, she was awarded a Nobel Peace Prize at the age of just 17. She has given speeches to the UN and met several world leaders to promote the causes of women's rights and global education. She continues to plan a future in politics. Malala Yousafzai's story has been profoundly affecting for women of all ages. Her courage in the face of evil, her suffering and her brilliance continue to astonish as she challenges the world to provide better opportunities and freedom for all.

Left: Malala Yousafzai speaks at the 'First Focus Event on Education' at the QEII Centre in central London, 2016

Above: Malala Yousafzai addresses young refugees at Kenya's Dadaab refugee complex during a visit organised by the UN High Commissioner for Refugees, 2016

CHAPTER 4:
Leaders and Politicians

Madeleine Albright

Born 1937 | American | Politician

The US has been surprisingly slow at elevating women to positions of political power, but a few exceptional individuals have penetrated the so-called 'glass ceiling'. The first woman to be Secretary of State was Madeleine Albright, a woman with an extensive knowledge of international affairs ranging across both trade and conflict situations. One conflict she particularly understood was World War II, having experienced it at first hand.

Albright, or Korbel as she was first called, was born in Prague, Czechoslovakia, just before the outbreak of World War II. Her parents fled to England when the Nazis invaded. They attempted to re-settle in Czechoslovakia after the war ended, but were forced to flee once more when Czechoslovakia became a puppet state of the Soviet Union. Albright's father became a successful academic at the University of Denver and Albright learned a great deal from him about international relations.

Albright attended university, where she was an able student. After graduating, she initially worked as a journalist, where she met her husband, Joseph Albright. She went back to college to study politics and Russian after her she had three children, gaining an MA and a PhD. She first worked as a political adviser for the Democrats in 1972, but her first role in international politics came in 1993 when President Clinton chose her to be the USA's permanent representative to the United Nations. Albright was a strong supporter of 'assertive multilateralism', so the role suited her well. She established a reputation as a no-nonsense individual who could tackle complex and delicate negotiations with a firm but fair hand.

In 1996, Albright's place in history was sealed when she was nominated as Secretary of State; the first woman to hold the position. In this role, Albright made a significant impact on world politics. A supporter of NATO (The North Atlantic Treaty Organization) and human rights, Albright attempted to broker peace in the Middle East and ushered in a new era of relative cooperation between the US and China. A believer in nuclear non-proliferation, Albright advocated for North Korea and Eastern Europe not to develop nuclear weapons and believed that the US should become positively involved in conflicts such as that in Kosovo, facilitating peace and helping victims. In 2000, she became the first Secretary of State to visit North Korea.

Since leaving politics in 2001, Albright has set up Albright Capital Management, a private investment fund which encourages private investment in countries from developing markets. She has also written a number of books, including memoirs of her years in politics such as *Madam Secretary: A Memoir* and an account of her childhood growing up in Czechoslovakia.

Albright has blazed a trail of competence and calm in the unstable and unpredictable arena of international relations. An icon for women in politics, she has led the way where many other women in US politics now seek to follow. She was awarded the Presidential Medal of Freedom in 2012 by Barack Obama.

Right: Madeleine Albright addresses the audience after being presented with the Department of Defense Medal for Distinguished Public Service, 2016

'I do believe that in order to be a successful negotiator that as a diplomat, you have to be able to put yourself into the other person's shoes. Unless you can understand what is motivating them, you are never going to be able to figure out how to solve a particular problem.'

Madeleine Albright

Left: Secretary of Defense, Ash Carter, presents former Secretary of State Madeleine Albright the Department of Defense Medal for Distinguished Public Service, on June 30, 2016 at the Pentagon in Arlington, Virginia

Top: Former National Security Advisor Stephen Hadley and former Secretary of State Madeleine Albright testified before the House Armed Services Committee about America's role in the world

Above: Former United States Secretaries of State Condoleezza Rice and Madeleine Albright attend the Watermark Conference for Women at San Jose Convention Center on February 1, 2017 in San Jose, California

Sirimavo Bandaranaike

1916–2000 | Sri Lankan | Politician

The first woman ever to lead an elected government, Sirimavo Bandaranaike was both a social reformer and a strong leader at a time of political instability and confrontation. Although her three periods as Prime Minister were not without controversy, she played an important role in shaping the role and identity of modern-day Sri Lanka in its transition from a British colony to an independent country.

Bandaranaike was born at a time when Ceylon (as Sri Lanka was formerly known), was under British rule. She was educated at a Convent School in Colombo but, unlike some born under British rule, was encouraged to maintain her Buddhist faith and to speak Sinhalese as well as English, thus maintaining a cultural connection with her own people. Many other Ceylonese from wealthy families had become highly anglicised under the rule of the British Empire and were considered distant from their compatriots.

After completing her education, Bandaranaike became well known for her independent acts of social welfare; delivering food and supplies to those in the countryside who struggled with poverty. In 1940 she married. Her husband was also from a wealthy and politically active family. He became Prime Minister in 1956 as leader of the Sri Lankan Freedom Party (SLFP). In 1959, however, he was assassinated at home and Sirimavo Bandaranaike was asked to continue as leader of the party in his place.

Although grieving at the time, she agreed. In 1960, during the country's elections, Bandaranaike's party won, making her the first elected female Prime Minister in the world.

Bandaranaike continued her husband's mainly socialist and nationalist politics, including the nationalisation of some large industries. Her support for the local Sinhalese language and culture, however, marginalised the Tamil minority who also lived in Ceylon. These became increasingly vocal and discontented about their exclusion from public life, especially after a repatriation deal with India broke down without completion, leaving many Tamils effectively stateless.

In 1965, amid political tensions, Bandaranaike lost the election, only to be re-elected in 1970 for a second term. Under this new government, formed as a socialist coalition, Bandaranaike's government introduced a new republican constitution under which the former Ceylon was named Sri Lanka. They also introduced economic policies intended to redistribute wealth towards the poorest. The coalition's socialist policies, however, led to some economic stagnation and Bandaranaike was replaced as Prime Minister in 1977.

Accusations of corruption and an increasingly dictatorial manner meant that Bandaranaike was stripped of her political rights in 1980, but pardoned in 1986 by President Jayawardene and restored to her political life. In the meantime, her son and daughter had also begun opposing political careers and her daughter Chandrika was elected Prime Minister as the head of her parents' party, the SLFP. When, in August 1994, Chandrika took the further step of becoming President, she asked her mother to become Prime Minister and work under her. Working with her daughter for the last years of her life, Bandaranaike withdrew from politics due to ill health in 2000 and died of a heart attack shortly afterwards.

In Bandaranaike's controversial career, she helped to usher the new Sri Lankan republic from the shadows of colonialism, but was short-sighted in her dealings with minorities in her own country. A fearsome fighter for justice, she could also be blind where justice was perhaps most necessary.

Bandaranaike was born at a time when Ceylon (as Sri Lanka was formerly known) was under British rule. She was educated at a Convent School in Colombo but unlike some born under British rule.

Right: Sirimavo Bandaranaike, the Prime Minister of Ceylon (later Sri Lanka), arrives at London Airport with her son Anura, to attend the Commonwealth Prime Ministers' Conference in London, 1961

Benazir Bhutto

1953–2007 | Pakistan | Prime Minister

Born into an influential political family, Benazir Bhutto seemed destined for a life of political power and turmoil, eventually becoming the first woman ever to head a Muslim-majority country and confounding tradition along the way. Her strength of character and desire to effect change in her own country are a monumental example of leadership and charisma. She was an inspiration to many women, including Malala Yousafzai, who later wore her shawl to the United Nations. In spite of the many setbacks she faced, her resolve never wavered; she was a leader to the end.

Her father Zulfikar was elected Prime Minister in 1973 as leader of the Pakistan People's Party (PPP), a socialist-progressive party which promoted greater equality and public ownership. At this time, Bhutto was studying at Harvard and Oxford, becoming President of the Oxford Union debating society. She completed her studies in 1976, intending to return and work in her father's government in the Pakistani Foreign Service.

When her father was overthrown by a military coup led by Muhammad Zia-ul-Haq and arrested in 1977, however, her life was thrown into chaos. She and her mother stayed in Pakistan to prepare her father's defence, in spite of being arrested themselves. When Zulfikar was finally convicted and executed in 1979, Bhutto and her mother became co-chairs of the PPP. Bhutto later formed the Movement for the Return to Democracy and called for an end to martial law, the restoration of the 1973 constitution, parliamentary elections and the transfer of political power from the military to the elected representatives.

Above: Benazir Bhutto denounces the arrest of her husband,
Asif Ali Zardari, as part of a plot to discredit the family, Pakistan, 1990

Left: Benazir Bhutto at Élysée Palace in Paris, France, 1989

Leaders and Politicians

Zia-ul-Haq responded by arresting and imprisoning Bhutto and her mother in 1981, after an organisation led by Bhutto's brothers organised a hijack in an attempt to oust the government. She was released and flown to England in 1984, where she began a self-imposed exile.

In 1985, martial law was lifted and Bhutto returned to Pakistan. She soon married Asif Ali Zardari in an arranged marriage organised by her mother. The marriage formed a rallying point for those still loyal to her father's party and in the election which followed in 1988, the PPP received the most votes. Benazir Bhutto became Prime Minister under President Khan; only the fourth ever female Prime Minister, and the first in a Muslim majority country. Her position was fragile, however, and the policies of privatisation that she promoted differed significantly from her father's socialist foundations. There were also many conservative Muslims who could not accept a woman as leader and the country struggled under divided regional and religious loyalties.

In 1990, President Khan dismissed Bhutto as Prime Minister after she tried to sideline him from major decisions. Her place was taken by opponent Nawaz Sharif, but after Sharif too clashed with President Khan, Bhutto and Sharif jointly ousted the President. In yet another election, Bhutto was again elected as Prime Minister under President Farooq Leghari.

As Prime Minister, Bhutto pursued policies of privatisation in an attempt to curb unemployment and ease poverty, but was less successful in implementing some of the measures for female equality that she had promised in her election campaigns. In 1996, her role as Prime Minister ended again amid accusations of corruption, after which she left to live in Dubai and Britain, but continued to lead the PPP from abroad.

After many years, the charges against Bhutto were dropped by President Musharraf and Bhutto's return to Pakistan in 2007 was greeted with delight by many, but with deadly intent by some. On 27th December 2007, Benazir Bhutto was assassinated by a suicide bomber believed to have been linked to the militant Islamic organisation, Al-Qaeda.

As Prime Minister, Bhutto pursued policies of privatisation in an attempt to curb unemployment and ease poverty, but was less successful in implementing some of the measures for female equality that she had promised in her election campaigns.

Right: Pakistan authorities release Benazir Bhutto, daughter of the late Zulfikar Ali Bhutto and herself now leader of political opposition to president Zia ul-Haq, 1986

Cleopatra

69–30 BCE | Greek | Egyptian monarch

It is difficult, peering through the murk of history, to feel a strong sense of Cleopatra's true nature, but history testifies to her ambition, courage and ability to charm as well as, perhaps, her greed and ruthlessness. Whatever the truth, she is undoubtedly the stuff of legend; depicted in plays, art, stories and films to the present day and certainly beyond.

The name Cleopatra is synonymous with beauty, power and bloody intrigue. The final ruler of Egypt before it was part of the Roman Empire, Cleopatra was born a direct descendant of the Greek Alexander the Great. Her full name was Cleopatra VII Philopator and she was a member of the Ptolemaic Dynasty. Although the family were Greek speaking, Cleopatra herself is said to have spoken Egyptian as well.

Cleopatra was made joint regent with her father at the age of 14, although her powers at that time were limited. When her father died, she married her brother Ptolemy XIII and became joint ruler with him as was the Egyptian custom. The union produced no heirs.

In 51 BCE, Cleopatra sidelined her brother from power and became the effective sole leader of Egypt, something that was not considered acceptable for a woman. Economic difficulties and internal struggles, however, led to Cleopatra being exiled in 48 BCE. In order to regain the throne of Egypt, she sought support from Julius Caesar, the Roman Emperor. Arriving at his palace secretly in a rolled up carpet, they began a relationship and nine months later Cleopatra gave birth to Caesar's child. He, supposedly besotted, supported her claim to the throne of Egypt. Caesar's forces attacked Ptolemy XIII at the Battle of the Nile and Ptolemy XIII was drowned.

Cleopatra took her even younger brother, Ptolemy XIV as co-ruler and resumed her rule of Egypt. The relationship between Cleopatra and Caesar continued until his assassination on 15th March 44 BCE, whereupon her position appeared more fragile. When Ptolemy XIV died, (possibly poisoned by Cleopatra,) she took her son Caesarion as her co-ruler.

She then became embroiled in the Roman Civil War which began between those who had assassinated Caesar and those who were loyal to him. Taking the side of those who were loyal to Caesar, she met with Mark Antony, who was one of three people ruling Rome at the time. He wanted her assurances of Egypt's loyalty, but in the course of negotiations the two also began a passionate relationship which lasted several years. The pair were married by Egyptian rite and had three children together: twins Alexander Helios and Cleopatra Selene II, and a further child called Ptolemy Philadelphus. Mark Antony eventually made Alexandria his home and their children were made rulers of regions of the Roman Empire including Armenia, Libya and Cyprus. During this time Egypt flourished and Cleopatra was considered by Egyptians to be the reincarnation of Isis, the mother-goddess.

Eventually, however, rivalries between Antony and Cleopatra and their opponents in Rome would come to a head. Mark Antony was defeated at the Battle of Actium and later committed suicide as Octavian invaded Egypt. Cleopatra's own suicide is well known, depicted in art and forming part of famous plays such as Shakespeare's *Antony and Cleopatra*. It is said that she allowed an asp to bite her so that she would die of its poison.

Above: Marble head of Cleopatra VII, Roman Civilisation, 50-30 BCE

Right: Elizabeth Taylor on the set of *Cleopatra*, 1963

Hillary Clinton

Born 1947 | American | Politician

A figure who has divided opinion, Hillary Clinton first became well known as the wife as President Bill Clinton, the 42nd President of the United States. A high-profile First Lady, Hillary was instantly recognised as a woman of substance in her own right. As a known political activist and legal expert, some questioned the role she played in politics as an unelected and unofficial adviser to the President. Many people, however, admired her ambition and her expertise and considered her a role model for women.

Her early life was quite different to the fame she has acquired in later life. The eldest daughter of a fabric store owner, Hillary grew up in a quiet suburb of Chicago. A star pupil throughout school, she eventually went on to study Law at Yale, graduating with honours. She was particularly interested in issues regarding children in the legal system.

Hillary was politically active throughout her education, initially supporting Republican causes and then changing her allegiance to the Democrats after hearing a speech by Martin Luther King Jr. After graduation, she worked in a number of minor political roles, including a stint as part of the presidential impeachment inquiry staff during the Watergate scandal.

After Nixon's resignation, Hillary went to Arkansas with her husband, where she resumed her legal career. Throughout this time, her political interests and affiliations became much clearer; Hillary was dedicated to the kind of public office that created equality of rights, opportunities and wealth. President Carter made her chairman of the Legal Services Corporation in return for her support for his presidential campaign. She also chaired the Arkansas Educational Standards Committee, co-founded the Arkansas Advocates for Children and Families and served on the boards of the Arkansas Children's Hospital, Arkansas Legal Services and the Children's Defence Fund in her role as 'first lady of the state' when Bill Clinton was elected as Governor of Arkansas.

Above and right: Hillary Clinton speaks at the Ms Foundation for Women 2017 Gloria Awards Gala and After Party at Capitale in New York City

Although her role as First Lady came to an end, Hillary continued her political career by being elected as Senator for New York in 1999.

Ms. FOUNDATION
FOR WOMEN

Leaders and Politicians

In 1993, Bill Clinton was elected President and Hillary's life took on a whole new level of public scrutiny. Seen as strong by some and too ambitious by others, Hillary nevertheless continued to fight for causes she believed in. In 1998, her life was overwhelmed by scandal when Bill was found to have had an affair with one of his interns. The marriage survived, but the affair caused many to regard Bill and Hillary's marriage as a marriage of political convenience to both parties.

Although her role as First Lady came to an end, Hillary continued her political career by being elected as Senator for New York in 1999. Many tipped her as a likely candidate for America's first female President and in 2007 it seemed as if this would indeed happen. Hillary was eventually beaten to the Democratic nomination by the up-and-coming Barack Obama and would have to wait eight more years for her next chance.

In 2016, it seemed as if fate was at last on Hillary's side. She won the Democratic nomination as the candidate for President and stood against the controversial and politically inexperienced Republican candidate Donald Trump in the Presidential election. Many viewed it as a foregone conclusion that Hillary Clinton would win – her political experience seemed to speak for itself. America, however, was changing. Many saw Hillary as tainted by the political establishment and by a narrow majority Trump won the election.

For Hillary, the only thing left to do was make her consolation speech as the losing candidate. For some, however, who admire her strength, knowledge and determination to be the USA's first female President, she will always be regarded as the rightful winner.

Right: Former US Secretary of State Hillary Clinton speaks during BookExpo 2017 at the Jacob K Javits Convention Center, New York City

Indira Gandhi

1917–1984 | Indian | Politician

Indira Gandhi was elected prime minister of India from 1966–1977 and again from 1980 until her assassination in 1984. She was India's first female Prime Minster. Politically left-leaning, she forged an alliance with the Soviet Union, led India to victory in the 1971 conflict with Pakistan, and established India as a nuclear power. Regarded by some as one of India's best Prime Ministers, Indira was a forceful politician who was not afraid to wield power. Critics argued that under her rule, power was too centralised and autocratic.

Gandhi was the only child of Jawaharlal Nehru, the leader of the Indian independence movement and, from 1947, the country's first Prime Minister. She attended Santiniketan University and Somerville College, Oxford, before marrying Feroze Gandhi in 1942. Shortly after their wedding, they were jailed for 13 months for taking part in a protest against British Rule in India. Both she and her husband would remain active in politics, however, with Feroze Gandhi winning a seat in the Indian parliament, while Indira became a personal advisor to her father. Feroze died in 1960, leaving her to raise two sons; Rajiv and Sanjay.

When Nehru died in 1964, Indira was persuaded to take up a career in politics herself. She was elected as a member of parliament in her father's Indian National Congress Party and was appointed a minister in the cabinet of Prime Minister Lal Bahadur Shastri. When Shastri died in office in 1966, Gandhi campaigned successfully to replace him as party leader and also as Prime Minister of India. As Prime Minister, Indira shrewdly used every political tool at her disposal to consolidate her power and authority.

Above: Indira Gandhi, prime minister of India, at the Commonwealth Prime Ministers' Conference at Marlborough House, London, 1969

Right: Indira Gandhi visiting Austria, Hotel Imperial in Vienna, 1983

'I am alive today, I may not be there tomorrow… I shall continue to serve until my last breath and when I die, I can say, that every drop of my blood will invigorate India and strengthen it.'

Indira Gandhi

Leaders and Politicians

In 1971, a hugely popular Gandhi won re-election but found herself charged with electoral fraud. In 1975, a high court upheld the charges and Gandhi lost her seat in parliament, as well as her role as Prime Minister. To prevent this, she began to rule by decree. Regarded as one of the darkest periods of Indian democracy, press was heavily censored and public opinion muted. During this period, Gandhi also implemented several unpopular policies, including sterilisation as a means of widespread birth control. In 1977, when she initiated new elections, she severely misjudged public reaction to her extreme actions and was voted out of office.

Gandhi returned to office as Prime Minister in 1980, amid turmoil in India as several states tried to gain independence from central government. In the Punjab, a Sikh majority began to demand greater political independence. The struggle turned ugly and in 1984 an armed Sikh freedom fighter group led by Jarnail Singh Bhindranwale barricaded itself inside the Golden Temple, Sikhism's holiest shrine. Following unsuccessful negotiations, Gandhi ordered the army to enter the temple and several hundred people were killed.

The event made Gandhi an enemy of many Sikhs. Five months later, Indira Gandhi was assassinated by two of her own Sikh bodyguards on 31st October 1984 as retaliation for her actions. In a quote made the day before she died, Gandhi seemed aware that her life may be at risk:

I am alive today, I may not be there tomorrow... I shall continue to serve until my last breath and when I die, I can say, that every drop of my blood will invigorate India and strengthen it.

Indira Gandhi

Ellen Johnson Sirleaf

Born 1938 | Liberian | President of Liberia

Nobel laureate, author and President of Liberia, Ellen Johnson Sirleaf has toiled through setbacks to be one of the most important women in the world. Sirleaf is a strong believer in the future potential of Africa and Liberia, the power of reconciliation and love to move a country forward. She believes in the essential nature of education and in the hidden power of women.

Born in 1938 in Monrovia, Sirleaf was married at the age of 17 and quickly had four children. She later travelled with her husband, James Sirleaf, a government employee, to the US so that she could continue her studies. In 1961, the couple divorced owing to James' abusive behaviour, but Sirleaf continued her studies, first in Madison Business College, then in the Economics Institute in Boulder, Colorado and finally at Harvard Business School.

On her return to Liberia in 1972, she was given a job as Assistant Minister of Finance under the administration of William Tolbert, and later was Minister of Finance, but was forced to flee the country after a military coup by Samuel Doe and fled to Washington, where she went to work for the World Bank. She later went to Nairobi to work as Vice President of the local branch of Citibank. In 1985, she ran for the role of Vice President in Liberia under President Jackson Doe, but was placed under house arrest for a speech in which she insulted the previous government. She was later released after international pressure on President Doe. Upon release, she ran instead for Senate and won, but refused to take up her seat as the entire national election had been judged fraudulent.

THE AFRICA-AMERICA INS
Educating People | Connecting

PRESENTING SPONSOR

Chevron

human energy

Left: Liberian President and Nobel Peace Prize laureate, Ellen Johnson Sirleaf attends a press conference in Monrovia, Liberia, 2014

Above: Ellen Johnson Sirleaf speaks onstage during the Africa-America Institute's 2016 Annual Awards Gala at Cipriani 25 Broadway, New York City

Leaders and Politicians

In 1989, civil war broke out in Liberia between President Doe and Charles Taylor. Sirleaf supported Taylor, but by 1996 had become critical of his methods and later left the country, after being defeated by Taylor in another fraudulent election.

Then in 2005, after further years of civil war, Sirleaf was finally elected President, standing for the Unity Party, a party which she hoped would bring together the opposing sides of the civil war. In her domestic policies she concentrated on reducing the national debt and has succeeded in having loans from the USA and other countries written off entirely. She also introduced free and compulsory education for all elementary age children and Africa's first freedom of information act. In 2006, she implemented the Truth and Reconciliation Commission, in order to bring to light acts of violence and corruption during 20 years of civil war. Unfortunately, when the Commission made its final report, it added Sirleaf to its list of people that should not practice in politics, owing to her short-lived support for Charles Taylor. Sirleaf apologised for this and pointed to her later criticism of him in mitigation. She continued as President.

In 2011, Sirleaf stood for re-election as President and at the same time was nominated for a Nobel Peace Prize for her efforts to bring Liberia together. She was awarded the Presidential Medal of Freedom in 2007 by George W Bush. She has encouraged foreign investment from other countries in Liberia. Increased education and investment have seen an improvement in living standards, especially in the provision of clean water in rural areas.

Her autobiography, *This Child will be Great: Memoir of a Remarkable Life by Africa's First Woman President*, tells her amazing story.

Above: Ellen Johnson Sirleaf attends the official release of the No Ceilings Full Participation Report in New York City, 2015

Right: Ellen Johnson Sirleaf and Barack Obama before Obama makes a statement to the news media in the White House, 2015, Washington, DC

'All girls know that they can be anything now. That transformation is to me one of the most satisfying things.'

Ellen Johnson Sirleaf

Angela Merkel

Born 1954 | German | Chancellor of Germany

Considered by many to be the most powerful woman in the world, Angela Merkel became leader of Germany in 2005. She has governed a powerful nation through times of extreme change, championed the cause of a united Europe and participated on the world stage with a controlled and intelligent manner which belies her fearlessness.

Of mixed German and Polish descent, Merkel was born in West Germany but moved to East Germany as an infant owing to her father's job as a pastor. Growing up in communist East Germany, Merkel, in common with all East German youth of her time, was expected to be a member of the FDJ or Free German Youth, the youth movement of the ruling Socialist Party. Membership of this organisation was officially voluntary, but it was understood that non-participation in the FDJ would make progression to higher education difficult.

Merkel studied Physics at the University of Leipzig for five years. At the end of this time she applied for an Assistant Professorship, but was told that she could only hold the post if she agreed to report the actions of fellow academics to the Stasi (secret police). Not wishing to become involved in this kind of espionage, Merkel declined. Instead, she became a researcher and completed her doctorate in quantum physics in 1986, while working at the Academy of Sciences in Berlin-Adlershof.

Merkel decided to enter politics in 1989 after the destruction of the Berlin Wall. From 1961 to 1989, East Germany had been divided from West Germany by a huge wall with guards posted at crossing points. Moving from one half of Germany to the other was forbidden and anyone crossing without permission could be shot. East Germany was led by a Socialist government strongly connected to the Soviet Union, while West Germany was led by a democratically elected government. When the wall was dismantled in 1989 amid great celebrations, the two halves of Germany quickly began to reunite. Merkel wanted to play a part in the unification. She joined a party called Democratic Awakening, which subsequently became part of the Christian Democratic Union of Germany.

Above: Angela Merkel at the third plenary session of the G20 summit in Hamburg, Germany, 2017

Above: French President Emmanuel Macron and Angela Merkel at the Élysée Presidential Palace, 2017 in Paris, France

Above: Merkel greets Chinese President Xi Jinping in Berlin, Germany, to open a panda exhibit at the Berlin Zoo before he attends the G20 economic summit, 2017

Left: Angela Merkel attends the G20 summit in Hamburg, Germany

In 1990, Merkel was elected to represent Stralsund – Nordvorpommern – Rügen in the Bundestag and was given the post of Minister for Women and Youth under Chancellor Helmut Köhl. Rising steadily through the ranks of the party, she was elected as leader of the Christian Democratic Union in 2000 and led the party until 2005, when she was elected as Chancellor of Germany at the head of a grand coalition.

Merkel's policies have involved a drive to cut public spending whilst raising public money through increases in VAT and the higher rate of taxation. Her government has overseen an increase in Germany's stability and prosperity. Perhaps her most controversial policy has been to allow the free movement of asylum seekers after the Syrian migrant crisis of 2015; a move which damaged her popularity at home, although it did demonstrate to the rest of the world how determined Merkel was to use Germany's wealth and power in the cause of compassion.

On the international stage, Merkel has proved a vastly important figure, pursuing a closer relationship with the US and providing the strongest guiding hand in the European Union. The senior politician within the G7 group of countries, she has met with the leaders of all major countries.

In her personal life, Merkel has been married twice: once briefly in her twenties and then again in 1998 to quantum physicist Joachim Sauer. She is a football fan and has retained the Christian faith she grew up with throughout her life.

Michelle Obama

Born 1964 | American | First Lady of the USA

Michelle Obama has become one of the most recognisable women in the world through her role as First Lady of the USA, but her talents, enterprises and interests extend well beyond this most public and exposed position. Michelle Obama's life before and since the White House has been characterised by a desire for social justice and an empathy with those whom the world does not naturally favour. She is a keen believer in ambition and aspiration for all individuals.

Born in Chicago, Obama's parents were not wealthy but were happy, united and highly supportive of their children; Michelle and her older brother Craig. Obama was a gifted child, following a scheme for gifted children and skipping second grade at school. She later earned a place at Princeton University to study sociology and from there went to Harvard to study law. It was in her first job with a law firm that she met her future husband, Barack Obama. Initially rejecting his request for a date because she had been assigned to mentor him, Michelle Obama soon changed her mind and the couple fell in love, marrying in 1992.

After beginning to date Barack, Michelle Obama left her private law firm to work in public service, taking on roles in the City of Chicago Mayor's office and the planning office. She also worked for a non-profit organisation supporting young people to train for public service jobs. In 1996, her career moved in another direction when she went to work for the University of Chicago as Dean of Student Services and then for the University of Chicago Medical Centre.

When Barack Obama began his political career, it quickly became apparent that his wife, Michelle Obama, was a considerable asset. She supported her husband with his

Above: Michelle Obama speaks during the Partnership for a Healthier America Summit, 2017 in Washington, DC

Right: Michelle Obama speaks onstage during MTV's 2017 College Signing Day With Michelle Obama at The Public Theater in New York City

'You may not always have a comfortable life and you will not always be able to solve all of the world's problems at once but don't ever underestimate the importance you can have because history has shown us that courage can be contagious and hope can take on a life of its own.'

Michelle Obama

Above: Michelle Obama makes one of her first public speeches at the Orlando Conference since leaving the White House

campaigning while still working herself. After Barack became President, Obama lent considerable support to a number of high profile campaigns as First Lady, mainly working on issues close to her heart: young people achieving their potential, health, childhood obesity, education and social justice.

Michelle's programme 'Let's Move' was aimed at promoting fitness through activity and sport. She also invited children into the White House to help her to create a vegetable garden and spoke widely about the importance of healthy food for children and adults, requesting that the White House kitchen serve organic food to guests. Talking about mental health issues, she emphasised the difficulty faced by some women who ran around after their families, never taking time for themselves. She has also highlighted the needs of families working within the armed forces.

Importantly, as a major figure in public life, Obama has never played down her role as a mother or diminished the importance of it. Michelle and Barack Obama's children, Malia and Sasha, were at the centre of family life in the White House. Michelle made sure of the fact that their lives as individuals would not be negatively affected by their father's or their mother's public roles.

Obama used the opportunity of being First Lady to make a number of important speeches, outlining her views on equality and social justice.

Top: Michelle Obama makes her last public remarks as First Lady, honouring the 2017 School Counselor of the Year

Above: US President Barack Obama and First Lady Michelle Obama stand for the National Anthem during the 2016 Kennedy Center Honors

Eva Perón (Evita)

1919–1952 | Argentinian | Politician

Immortalised in a 1979 by the stage musical 'Evita', Eva Perón's short and extraordinary life was more dramatic than any stage show could convey.

Eva was born illegitimately in 1919. Her father, the wealthy but unfaithful Juan Duarte, returned to his legitimate family when Eva was one year old, leaving Eva and her family in desperate poverty and isolated by disgrace. Eva's mother, Juana Ibarguren, moved the family to a one-room apartment in a poor and dusty village called Los Toldos. There, she mended clothes to feed the family. Eva and her brothers and sisters also worked when they were old enough.

Eva enjoyed performing and taking part in school plays. As the family began to prosper, the cinema became Eva's favourite entertainment. At the tender age of 15, she ran away to Buenos Aires, in those days known as the 'Paris of South America', to begin a career on the stage.

Finding success in a new city must have been an immense challenge and there are rumours about Eva's affairs with influential men. She soon found work as an actress in films and on the radio. Although not a huge star, she signed a five-year contract to perform in a radio series called *Great Women of History* and it was through her acting work that Eva met her future husband, politician Juan Perón.

In 1944, Juan Perón was the Argentinian Secretary of Labour. At a time of political schism between the bourgeoisie and the poor working classes in Argentina, he had become a figurehead for the poor. When he organised a gala concert to raise money for victims of a major earthquake in San Juan, Eva was part of the line-up. Although Perón was almost twice her age, they became immediately attracted to one another.

Perón's power and influence was rising, but he was making enemies among the traditional, wealthy Argentinians. In October 1945, he was imprisoned by those who were afraid of his influence over the poor and feared an uprising. Just eight days later, however, more than a quarter of a million ordinary people gathered outside the Casa Rosada to demand his release and their wish was granted. After this, powerful and rich Perón courted scandal when he married the illegitimate and poorly educated Eva who had supported him through the ordeal. Although controversial, it was also to prove a highly successful move for both of them. Eva's poor upbringing meant that the ordinary people of Argentina took her to their heart; she could speak for them with genuine understanding.

In 1946, Eva Perón campaigned alongside her husband for his presidential election. He won by a landslide and Eva herself became heavily involved in political causes, working as a minister for health and labour. She founded the Eva Perón Foundation as an attempt to improve the country's antiquated welfare system. Hugely popular for her work among the 'descamisados' (literally 'shirtless ones'), she also stood up for the rights of poor women, fighting for female suffrage and better healthcare. Eva herself became a symbol of female emancipation, taking on responsible roles and working as many as 20 hours each day.

In 1952, Juan Perón ran for re-election and Eva Perón stood for Vice President, but she died suddenly of cancer at the age of 33. The nation mourned terribly for the loss of 'Evita' at her state funeral and for many years after. Her name has become symbolic around the world as a fighter for justice and the poor of Argentina.

Right: Eva Duarte Perón, popularly known as 'Evita', holding her pet dog at her home in Olivos, a suburb of Buenos Aires

Eleanor Roosevelt

1884–1962 | American | Humanitarian and First Lady of the USA

Aside from her role providing essential support to causes such as the civil rights movement and women's rights at the very heart of government, Eleanor Roosevelt's legacy is as a leading influence on the birth of human rights for all, forever. She also provided the world with some brilliant philosophical quotes.

Eleanor was born in New York City to a wealthy family; in fact, her uncle Theodore Roosevelt was the 26th President of the USA. However, both Eleanor's parents died by the time she was 10, leaving her to be brought up by her maternal grandmother.

In 1889, Eleanor was sent to school at Allenswood Academy in England, where she encountered feminist and independent thinking. Back in the US, she married her distant cousin Franklin in 1905 and they had six children. Although the marriage was a happy one, it came close to collapse in 1918 when Eleanor discovered that her husband had been having an affair with Lucy Mercer, her social secretary.

Franklin suffered from extreme ill health in 1921, but Eleanor actively encouraged him to return to public life and supported him throughout the rest of his political career.

During the 1920s, she became actively involved with social affairs, a cause which was to dominate much of her life from that point onwards and which was often useful in supporting her husband's political and economic ambitions. During the 1920s she worked with the Women's Trade Union League supporting its campaigns against child labour, a reduced working week and a minimum wage. She also fostered closer links with other women in the Democratic Party, which undoubtedly aided Franklin's eventual electoral success.

Historically, the role of the First Lady was largely ceremonial. Eleanor, however, brought considerable energy to the position but courted controversy at the same time. In particular, she was prominent in her support of the civil rights movement in which the black minority demanded improvements to their legal rights.

Her activity increased immeasurably after the US entered World War II in 1941. She became Assistant Director of the Office of Civilian Defence and travelled widely to wartime conferences. She was also a leading light in the promotion of the rights of women and African Americans during the war, most notably supporting the Tuskegee Airmen in their attempt to become the first black combat pilots.

'Do what you feel in your heart to be right for you'll be criticized anyway. You'll be damned if you do, and damned if you don't.'

Eleanor Roosevelt

Leaders and Politicians

Arguably, however, her greatest contribution was to come after her husband's death, in her role as US representative to the newly formed United Nations between 1946 and 1952. Invited to take the position by President Harry S Truman, she was to be a highly influential figure during these formative years. She was the first chairman of the UN Human Rights Commission and was one of those who drafted the UN's Universal Declaration of Human Rights, adopted by the General Assembly in December 1948.

Leaving her post at the UN in 1953 following the election of President Eisenhower, she continued to be active in liberal politics, supporting the New Deal Coalition and women's rights, although she opposed the Equal Rights Amendment, believing that it would not positively improve the position of women in US society. Her last public role, held between 1961 and her death the following year, was as chairman of the Presidential Commission on the Status of Women, a role to which she had been invited by Present John F Kennedy.

Right: American humanitarian and social activist, Eleanor Roosevelt

Below: Eleanor Roosevelt holds up a copy of 'The Universal Declaration of Human Rights', circa 1947

Margaret Thatcher

1925–2013 | British | Prime Minister

In 1979, Margaret Thatcher became the first female Prime Minister of Great Britain. In doing so, she became an icon for women all over the world. Thatcher's conservative policies were a controversial mix of downsizing the government and making individuals responsible for their own well-being. She believed that state intervention in people's lives should be kept to a minimum.

Born on 13th October 1925 as the daughter of a grocer, Thatcher graduated from Oxford University with a chemistry degree and later studied law. She became involved in politics at the age of 25 and was MP for Finchley at 33, gaining a seat in the shadow cabinet just two years later. She enjoyed a long and devoted marriage to Denis and had two children, Carol and Mark.

Thatcher's policies were in many ways the result of the 1970s economic crisis. In 1975, Thatcher was elected leader of the Conservative Party, defeating Ted Heath. In doing so, she became the first woman leader of a major British political party. At the time, Britain was governed by a Labour Government under James Callaghan. Owing to global events such as the OPEC oil crisis, inflation was high, which caused a fall in the value of Sterling. When the International Monetary Fund urged Britain to keep inflation under control, the Labour Party introduced deep cuts in public spending, especially on education and health.

This led to a period of strikes and public dissatisfaction known as the 'winter of discontent'. In 1979, the Labour Prime Minister James Callaghan was easily defeated by Margaret Thatcher's Conservative Party in the General Election. People felt that the unions and the strikers had too much power and had made their lives too miserable. The British public wanted change.

Right: British Prime Minister Margaret Thatcher outside a polling station in London during London borough council elections, 1990

Far right: Margaret Thatcher stands, arms raised, at a Conservative Party conference in Brighton; the IRA tried to assassinate her earlier that day

If change was what the public wanted, that's exactly what they got. Thatcher's government embarked on an economic program called Monetarism. Taxes were slashed so that people had more money in their pockets, but the smaller income for the government led to a period of 'rationalisation' or privatisation. Thatcher believed the country had become bloated with state-controlled, unprofitable industries such as the coal mines, steel, gas, electrics and telecommunications. One by one, she sold off these industries to be run as Public Limited Corporations and the public were invited to buy shares.

She also took a hard line with strikers and refused their demands. The most significant confrontation against strikers was with the miners. As pits were closed and jobs lost, striking miners felt savagely mistreated as their way of life and their communities were dismantled.

Thatcher won three general elections, the second in 1983 after successfully defending the Falkland Islands and the third in 1987 after keeping Britain out of Europe's Exchange Rate

Mechanism. This made her the longest serving Prime Minster in 100 years. Shortly after her third electoral victory, however, she presided over the introduction of the Community Charge or Poll Tax, a system of taxation that many felt was deeply unfair to the poor. Demonstrations followed and people began to feel that Margaret Thatcher was losing touch with her party and the public.

In 1990, following a rebellion within her cabinet, she resigned from office and in 1992 left the House of Commons altogether. When she died in April 2013, her death was accompanied by fierce debate about how she should be remembered; a courageous reformer or a destructive, power-crazed villain. Margaret Thatcher divided opinion throughout her life and even after her death.

Above: Margaret Thatcher, with husband Denis, waves to well-wishers outside Number 10 Downing Street following her election victory, on May 4, 1979

Left: Margaret Thatcher, interviewed by French weekly news magazine 'L'Express' in 198

Elizabeth I

1533–1605 | British | Queen of England

Although Elizabeth was born into a royal household as the daughter of the King of England, her life was full of challenges both political and personal. Many rulers before her had been removed and killed by rivals and it was only by intelligence, diplomacy and courage that Elizabeth was able to survive some 44 years as Queen of England. Her reign was not only long but successful, bringing victory in battle, a flourishing of culture of creativity and some religious stability to a divided England.

Elizabeth was the daughter of King Henry VIII and his second wife Anne Boleyn. Anne was beheaded when Elizabeth was just two and a half years old, but Elizabeth continued to be brought up in the royal court along with her older sister Mary, whose mother was also dead. Although they were Henry's children, they were both declared illegitimate, unable to inherit the throne.

When Henry VIII died, his young son Edward VI ascended the throne, but died six years later at the age of just 15. This led to a power struggle after which Mary ascended the throne. At this time, England was heavily divided between Catholics and Protestants. Elizabeth was a Protestant while Mary, her sister and Queen, was a Catholic. English Protestants strongly favoured a challenge to the throne by Elizabeth, but in the end none came: Mary handed the throne to Elizabeth when she died in 1558.

Elizabeth's initial method of government was to keep England out of trouble. She ended war with the French in order to spend less of the nation's capital and for the majority of her reign avoided war with Spain, although she was required to defend the country from the Spanish Armada in 1588 – a battle from which she emerged victorious.

Although she was moderate in her relations with the Catholics and didn't engage in the same level of persecution that Mary had directed at Protestants, she established the Church of England more securely than her father had done and made the method of worship across the country consistent by bringing back the Common Book of Prayer.

'I know I have the body of a weak and feeble woman but I have the heart and stomach of a king, and a King of England, too.'

Elizabeth I

Above: The signature of Queen Elizabeth I

Right: Portrait of Elizabeth I, wearing rich clothing classic of the era to which she lent her name

Leaders and Politicians

The Elizabethan age is seen as a time of cultural development: great explorers like Sir Walter Raleigh and Sir Francis Drake travelled the seas, bringing back new goods and wonderful tales; some of the world's greatest literature was written, such as the early plays of William Shakespeare. The poet Edmund Spenser wrote a poem called 'The Faerie Queen' which was dedicated to Elizabeth and Elizabeth employed musicians such as Thomas Tallis in her court.

In spite of many offers, Elizabeth never married and in fact cultivated an image of herself as the 'Virgin Queen' working hard for her people. She seemed to have a special interest in Robert Dudley, a member of her court, but the relationship never developed even after the mysterious death of Dudley's wife and the Queen seemed happy to rule alone.

Elizabeth died in 1603. In death, she left the throne to James I and united England with Scotland under one ruler.

Right: Stone marking the Tudor Palace of Greenwich

...OOR PALACE OF GREENWICH
...HPLACE
OF
... HENRY VIII
... IN 1491
...HIS DAUGHTERS
...EN MARY I IN 1516
AND
...UEEN ELIZABETH I
IN 1533

...LT BY KING HENRY VII

CHAPTER 5:
Sport
and
Entertainment

Audrey Hepburn

1929–1993 | British-Belgian-American | Actress

Although Hepburn is known for being one of the 20th century's great beauties, she had a considerable talent for acting and in later life achieved the greatest fulfilment through her gruelling humanitarian work. She even became a role model for the idea of aging gracefully, telling one photographer who came to take shots of her for an interview that he must not airbrush out her wrinkles because she had 'earned every one of them'.

Audrey Hepburn was British by nationality, but during her childhood moved around between Belgium, Britain and The Netherlands. Her father, Joseph Ruston, was a wealthy businessman and her mother was a Dutch baroness. Although Hepburn's childhood was privileged, it was disrupted by the departure of her father when she was six years old.

At the outbreak of war in 1939, Hepburn's mother moved from England to The Netherlands, where she believed the war would be less likely to affect them. Her gamble proved a poor one, as the Nazis invaded The Netherlands in 1940. Hepburn's uncle was executed in 1942 and her half-brother was sent to a labour camp. By the end of the war, the family were virtually starving along with many others in the Netherlands.

After the war, Hepburn and her mother moved back to England and Hepburn resumed her training as a ballerina. She left to concentrate on her film career, however, after being told that her height and the ill health she had suffered as the result of malnutrition during the war meant that she would never achieve her ambition of being a prima ballerina.

Above and right: Portrait and headshot of Belgian-born actress Audrey Hepburn as she sits by a stone wall, 1950s

'The "Third World" is a term I don't like very much, because we're all one world. I want people to know that the largest part of humanity is suffering.'

Audrey Hepburn

Sport and Entertainment

Hepburn's big break came when she was asked to play the lead role in the stage version of *Gigi* on Broadway. Then in 1953, she had her first starring film role when she was cast as Princess Ann in *Roman Holiday*. The film was a box office hit and Hepburn received a BAFTA, an Academy Award and a Golden Globe for her performance.

Perhaps her most well known performances, however, were as Holly Golightly in *Breakfast at Tiffany's* and as Eliza in *My Fair Lady*. Her iconic performance in *Breakfast at Tiffany's* opposite George Peppard was not only a box-office success but also a high point in 1960s fashion. In *My Fair Lady*, Hepburn was upset when her singing, for which she had received special training, was dubbed over by another singer, Marni Nixon. She briefly stormed off the set and the film seemed in doubt, but when the film was released her acting performance was a triumph.

In her private life Hepburn was married twice: first to actor Mel Ferrer and then to psychiatrist Andrea Dotti. In the final years of her life, which she described as the happiest, she lived with partner Robert Wolders. She had two children but was plagued by miscarriages until her mid-forties.

In her late fifties, Hepburn undertook work as a Goodwill Ambassador for UNICEF; a role which took her to some of the most difficult and distressing areas of the world. Encouraged by her own memories of malnutrition as a child, she used her position to draw attention to the conditions of suffering children. She was critical of the actions of politicians, who ignored the humanitarian interests of their countries in order to further political ends: 'The "Third World" is a term I don't like very much, because we're all one world. I want people to know that the largest part of humanity is suffering.'

Hepburn was awarded the Presidential Medal of Freedom by George H W Bush, in recognition of her humanitarian work with UNICEF.

Above and left: Hepburn's trademark image made her instantly recognisable in a number of film roles

Katharine Hepburn

1907–2003 | American | Actress

Hepburn is known for her many remarkable acting performances throughout the 20th century, but her impact on the film industry extends well beyond her acting. Outspoken and at times unpopular, Hepburn pushed the boundaries of female behaviour and refused to conform to the norms of stereotypical femininity that were demanded of women in the public eye.

Born to unconventional and progressive parents in Conneticut, Hepburn was encouraged to develop in any way she could, with none of the usual restrictions placed on her because of gender that were typical in the early 20th century. She accompanied her mother on suffrage marches, took part in athletics and attended university. She was very badly affected by the apparent suicide of her older brother Tom when she was 14 and struggled with her studies and social activities for several years.

After graduation, Hepburn immediately went away to begin her career in the theatre. Her early years were not marked with success, but in 1932 she became a Broadway success for her role in *The Warrior Husband*. A film career quickly followed and by 1933 she had received her first academy award for her performance in *Morning Glory*. She won further awards for her performance as Jo in *Little Women*. Hepburn's performances were striking for the unusual characterisation that she brought to them. One reviewer at the time said of her that she was 'a distinct, definite, positive personality.'

Following this success were several years of commercial failure at the hands of feckless producers and poor directors and she was eventually labelled 'box office poison'. Hepburn, however, was determined to take control of her own career and bought out her own contract from movie company RKO. Instead of continuing to play in unsuccessful films, she took a role in a stage play, *The Philadelphia Story*, which she could tailor as a vehicle for herself. She bought the film rights and eventually sold them to MGM, with herself as producer and her choice of co-stars. This marked the beginning of her rehabilitation as a star in the eyes of the public and the film industry alike.

When Hepburn reached her forties, an age when most actresses known for beauty were often seen to retire, she instead took on new challenges which revealed her artistic ability for its true worth. Hepburn took on Shakespearean roles such as Rosalind in *As You Like It* and in 1951 made one of her most significant successes, *The African Queen*, in which she played a middle-aged and cantankerous spinster. A further role as a spinster who has a passionate affair in *Summertime* showed Hepburn's skill in understanding and portraying this particular period of her life.

Hepburn continued to act with continued success until well into her seventies, taking on roles as diverse as Cleopatra and Coco Chanel. She avoided the film industry machine, rarely giving interviews until later in her career and not appearing at award ceremonies. Her only long relationship was with long-term co-star Spencer Tracy, with whom she was 'blindingly in love', but the couple never married as Tracy was reluctant to seek a divorce from his estranged wife. The unconventional nature of the relationship is a reflection of Hepburn's rejection of societal norms.

Outspoken and at times unpopular, Hepburn pushed the boundaries of female behaviour, and refused to conform to the norms of stereotypical femininity that were demanded of women in the public eye.

Left: Portrait of Katharine Hepburn; she owed her success as an actress to her bravery to take control in a male-dominated industry

Billie Jean King

Born 1943 | American | Tennis Player

Tough and competitive, Billie Jean King swept the world of women's sport into a new phase. She demanded more respect and support for women in sport and changed their earning potential forever. In later life she has become a vocal supporter of gay and lesbian rights.

Billie Jean King (born Billie Jean Moffitt) grew up in Long Beach, California, into a stable, traditional family. All of the family was heavily involved in sports: Billie Jean's mother was a swimmer, her father an athlete and her brother was a baseball player who would later turn professional. At the age of 11, King tried tennis, at first receiving free coaching. This became her sport of choice.

An aggressive and highly competitive player from an early age, King quickly began winning local tournaments and entered her first USA Grand Slam event in 1959 at the age of 15, where she lost in the first round. For the next few years King gradually learned her craft, travelling the world, sometimes winning and often losing.

In 1965, however, things began to go her way. Ranked as the USA's number one player, King became only the fifth woman in history to achieve a career Grand Slam (winning all the major titles). She achieved 39 Grand Slam titles in total. As an opponent, she was mentally tough and would charge to the net and intimidate her opponents.

In 1973, King famously took part in the 'Battle of the Sexes'. This was an exhibition match against Bobby Riggs, a former men's number one, to see whether a woman could beat a man. King did win; earning $100,000 and a lot of respect.

Off the court, King was frustrated by the lack of respect given to female tennis players and the inequality between their earnings and those of male players. In the 1970s, she helped to organise and support the first women's professional tennis tour and became President of the Women's Tennis Association.

Tough and competitive, Billie Jean King swept the world of women's sport into a new phase. She demanded more respect and support for women in sport and changed their earning potential forever.

Left: Tennis legend Billie Jean King speaks at the ANA Inspiring Women in Sports Conference

Sport and Entertainment

Many of King's efforts at raising the profile of female tennis players were supported by her husband, Larry King. The couple married in 1965, but as the years went by, King began to realise that she was attracted to women. She began a secret relationship with her secretary, Marilyn Barnett, but when the relationship ended, King was publicly 'outed' in court by Barnett. This was difficult for King as she had been unable to discuss the relationship with her own family and homosexuality was not, at the time, widely accepted:

'I wanted to tell the truth but my parents were homophobic and I was in the closet.'

King lost all her sponsorship money and had to give Barnett so much money in court that she was forced to continue her playing career whether she wanted to or not.

After her initial difficulties in acknowledging her sexuality openly, King became a leading advocate for gay and lesbian rights, as well as championing the cause of women in sport. She was awarded the Presidential Medal of Freedom by Barack Obama for her work on behalf of girls and women, and the gay and lesbian and transgender community. He said:

'This is a chance for me – and for the United States of America – to say thank you to some of the finest citizens of this country and of all countries.'

Above: Emma Stone and Billie Jean King pose with Trailblazer Award at the 2016 Logo's Trailblazer Honors

Above: Billie Jean King looks on before opening the roof during an event at Arthur Ashe Stadium in August, 2016

Esther Rantzen

Born 1940 | British | TV Presenter

Through her career in television and journalism, Rantzen has become a fighter for difficult causes and the defenceless. She made a number of pioneering programmes on child birth, mental health, drug abuse and child abuse. In 1986, she founded ChildLine, a children's helpline that allows children facing difficult situations such as abuse or neglect to ring in and talk to someone. She is a trained volunteer counsellor and, since the merger of ChildLine with the NSPCC, has been a Trustee of the organisation. More recently, she founded the charity The Silver Line.

Born in 1940, Rantzen was brought up in a middle-class North London family and was privately educated, before continuing her education at Somerville College, Oxford. She joined the BBC to train as a secretary but quickly moved on to other things. Esther's journalistic career began with BBC Radio as a sound effects assistant. From there, she moved into television as a reporter on lifestyle and consumer shows.

In 1973, she became a household name as the presenter of *That's Life*, which ran for 21 years and regularly drew audiences of over 18 million viewers. The show was dominated by consumer affairs but also ran famous campaigns into issues such as organ donation and child abuse. Some of the sensitive stories that Rantzen covered became major national talking points. The show also varied its content with amusing songs and tales from real life. Some now-famous names, such as Victoria Wood, made their debuts on *That's Life*.

Much of Rantzen's journalistic work could be characterised as an exploration of her own life, followed by attempts to use her experiences for the benefit of others. In 2011, after the death of her husband Desmond Wilcox, Rantzen began exploring topics related to old age and wrote an article for the *Daily Mail* about loneliness. The response from older people wanting to open up about the problem was overwhelming and, in 2012, The Silver Line was born. The Silver Line is a charity where older people can call in for a conversation or to tell someone how they are feeling. She has also written news articles and given interviews about other issues she has encountered in her own life, such as becoming a mother late in life.

Rantzen is a patron of a number of charities and helped to found the Association of Young People with ME/CFS, of which she is President. Her daughter has struggled with the condition and having been involved in it first hand, Rantzen wanted to raise awareness for the benefit of all young sufferers.

In 2013, Esther became known to a younger audience when she appeared on ITV1's *I'm a Celebrity, Get Me Out of Here!* where her mature wisdom was appreciated by her fellow campers.

In another change of direction, Rantzen stood at the 2010 General Election as an Independent candidate for Luton South, in protest at the incumbent MPs expenses claims, which had become a national scandal. She lost the vote.

Rantzen has received a number of awards including an OBE, a CBE and a DBE for services to children and older people through ChildLine and The Silver Line. She received the Royal Television Society's Special Judges' Award for Journalism and was received into their Hall of Fame. In addition, she was the first woman to receive the Dimbleby award from BAFTA for her on-screen television work, the Lifetime Achievement Award from Women in Film and Television and the Snowdon award for services to disabled people. Esther has six honorary doctorates and has been made an honorary Fellow of Somerville College.

Right: Dame Esther Rantzen attends The Pride of Britain Awards 2016

Sister Rosetta Tharpe

1915–1973 | American | Singer

Considered a musical prodigy at the age of 4, Sister Rosetta Tharpe caused an earthquake in the world of popular music. Trained as a gospel singer, Tharpe's keyboard skills, guitar playing and singing created a style of music and musicianship which have influenced many major singers and performers since, including Elvis Presley, Eric Clapton and Chuck Berry. Her achievements and popularity are particularly surprising as she was born at a time when there was widespread inequality between men and women and when many black people in America still suffered racial segregation. Her musical ability and personal magnetism was such that people couldn't stay away.

Born Rosetta Nubin, Tharpe's mother Katie Bell was an established singer and preacher with the Church of God in Christ, a church in which musical expression played a central role. Katie Bell encouraged Tharpe to play the guitar almost as soon as she was able to walk and the child quickly came to join her mother as a gospel performer on stage, touring around the US and playing evangelical music to large crowds. Rosetta married a man called Thomas Thorpe at the age of 19 and although the marriage didn't last, she kept a variant of her married name as her stage name.

Above and right: Sister Rosetta Tharpe poses for a portrait holding a guitar, circa 1940; she would later influence rock legends such as Elvis Presley, Eric Clapton and Chuck Berry

'She would sing until you cried and then she would sing until you danced for joy. She helped to keep the church alive and the saints rejoicing.'

Epitaph of Sister Rosetta Tharpe

Sport and Entertainment

In 1938, Tharpe moved to New York City and signed with Decca Records. She recorded four gospel songs in quick succession and all of them were hits. Later in the same year, Tharpe performed her unique style of gospel with blues and swing at Carnegie Hall. It was still considered unseemly at the time for a woman to publicly play the guitar and her performance both shocked and thrilled the audience, adding to Tharpe's fame. She also performed at the famous Cotton Club. When America joined the war in the 1940s, Tharpe was one of only two African Americans to be asked to record songs for the troops serving abroad, or 'V' discs as they were known; a sign of her considerable crossover appeal to both black and white music lovers.

Also in the 1940s, Tharpe teamed up with Sammy Price for two unusual arrangements of guitar, piano and gospel music, although these were condemned by her religious fans who believed they were 'the devil's music'. Following this criticism, Tharpe formed a duet with fellow gospel singer Maria Knight, and the two collaborated successfully on a number of gospel recordings. In 1951, Tharpe married Russell Morrison at a lavish ceremony in Griffith Stadium at which 25,000 were present. The event finished with a concert and a firework display.

A downturn in Tharpe's professional life came when she decided to make a secular album with Maria Knight. This blues album drew widespread condemnation from Tharpe's religious fan base, who felt that she had abandoned her beliefs. Although she never recovered her former popularity, Tharpe continued to record and tour until her death from a stroke in 1973. Her legacy to music is unfathomable; not only did she inspire a generation of rock and roll artists, she blazed a trail for women to express themselves freely through music.

Above: Sister Rosetta Tharpe waves as she arrives at London Airport, 1957

Right: Sister Rosetta Tharpe performing on stage

Emma Watson

Born 1990 | British | Actress and UNICEF Ambassador

Emma Watson first appeared on screen as Hermione Granger in the blockbuster *Harry Potter* movies at the age of 10. A critical success from the start of her career, her role as Hermione saw her given several awards including several Otto awards and Child Performer of the Year. She has since gone on to represent UNICEF as a Goodwill Ambassador.

Having visited developing nations in her support for female education and women's rights, Watson's young voice has become a welcome addition to a conversation that has been happening for far too long; women's rights – or the lack of them – have been a subject of discussion for over 150 years. Watson has received widespread recognition for her work, being named Female Celebrity of the Year in 2014 and number 26 on the *TIMES* 'Most important 100 people'. While some might say the global fight for women's rights is a huge task for a young woman, she is totally committed.

Watson was born in Paris but raised in Oxford after her lawyer parents separated. Leading a comfortable, middle-class life, Watson trained as an actor at the local Stagecoach drama school. During the filming of *Harry Potter*, she and the other child actors were largely taught by a tutor. When the final films were made, Watson was at university in Rhode Island and Oxford, but had to take some breaks to allow for filming.

Watson's first film, *Harry Potter and the Philosopher's Stone*, saw Watson and her young co-stars: Daniel Radcliffe and Rupert Grint, thrust into the limelight at a young age and bequeathed the tricky business of growing up in public. Each of them has handled the unusual level of attention in their own way, forging independent acting careers on stage and screen beyond the original series of *Harry Potter* films.

Watson's performances since *Harry Potter* have included *The Perks of Being a Wallflower* and Belle in the live action movie of *Beauty and the Beast*, as well as numerous other supporting roles on film, stage and television. Faced with the tricky task of making new roles believable when she is so well known as Hermione, Watson has received good reviews and has successfully made the transition to being judged as an adult actress. She has also worked as a model and featured on the cover of *Vogue*.

In a new and important chapter of her life, Watson was appointed a Goodwill Ambassador for the UN on women's issues and launched a new campaign called *HeforShe*, in which men are encouraged to stand up for women's rights alongside women. It is an issue that has been close to her heart since her childhood, when she recalls being called 'bossy' for behaving in the same way as her male peers, and being sexualised by the press at the age of 14.

'Call me a 'diva', call me a 'feminazi', call me 'difficult', call me a 'First World feminist', call me whatever you want, it's not going to stop me from trying to do the right thing and make sure that the right thing happens. Because it doesn't just affect me, it affects all the other women who are in this with me, and it affects all the other men who are in this with me, too.'

Emma Watson

Left: Actress Emma Watson attends *The Circle* screening during 2017 Tribecca Film Festival in New York City

Serena Williams

Born 1981 | American | Tennis Player

Although some people find Williams' overt self-confidence hard to take, she has earned the right to be confident through hard work and determination. In a world where women are still often expected to be 'nice' and not 'show off', Williams' attitude should be seen as a redefinition of what womanhood can be. In an awesome series of achievements, Williams has set new standards for female athleticism as well as mental toughness. Her glittering tennis career has seen her win more Grand Slam titles than any other female player, but this seems to be only the beginning of her talents and aspirations. Recent years have seen her branching out into other areas such as fashion, film and philanthropy.

Williams grew up in Compton, California, an area deliberately chosen by her father because of its reputation for deprivation and gang violence. Although an intelligent, law-abiding man, Williams' father, Richard, wanted his daughters to see for themselves what happens to people who do not receive or use their education; he wanted to drive them to be better than this environment. Although Williams was one of five sisters, only she and her older sister Venus were trained in tennis by their father. Williams began two-hour coaching sessions with him at the age of three, progressing through local and children's tournaments before she was 10.

Williams entered her first professional tournament at the age of 14, but by the time she graduated high school three years later, had achieved sufficient status to be offered a giant sponsorship deal. She won her first Grand Slam tournament at the age of 17, beating her sister Venus in the final of the US Open. In spite of their obvious sporting rivalry, Serena and Venus Williams have remained extremely close throughout their lives, living together for 12 years and taking on joint financial and charitable projects. Serena has said of Venus, 'She is my inspiration. She is my only reason.'

More titles were to follow, with both Serena and Venus becoming two of the biggest stars of the sport. Williams achieved her career Grand Slam and held all four Grand Slam titles simultaneously. There were problems too, however. She suffered a knee injury in 2003 and in the same year her older sister Yetunde was tragically murdered; an event which left the whole family in a state of shock. The following three years saw a slump in Williams' fortunes and her tennis ranking fell as she struggled for form and motivation.

Many doubted that she would return to tennis, but the doubters were proved wrong in dramatic style. By 2009, Williams was back in the top rankings and continued winning tournaments until achieving her 23rd record-breaking Grand Slam win in 2016. The following year, Williams gave birth to a baby girl, the pregnancy having already begun during Williams' final victorious tournament.

The inequalities that Williams witnessed in her early life have clearly remained an important influence on her; in 2009, Williams founded the Serena Williams Foundation with the aim of 'creating equity through education and assisting victims of senseless violence'. She has seen through a number of projects, including building new schools in Africa and kitting out schools in her home town of Compton. She has also opened a support centre for the victims of violence in a clear effort to prevent attacks like the murder of her sister and to support families who suffer as a result of similar tragedies.

'I'm really exciting. I smile a lot, I win a lot, and I'm really sexy.'

Serena Williams

Right: Serena Williams celebrates victory during the Ladies Singles second round match on day five of the Wimbledon Lawn Tennis Championships, 2016

Oprah Winfrey

Born 1954 | American | TV Presenter and Talk Show Host

She has been called the most influential woman in the world, was the wealthiest African American of the 20th century and was the USA's first black multi-billionaire, which is an impressive list of achievements for a woman who started life so poor that her grandmother had to dress her in old sacks. This is the wonder of Oprah; a rags to riches story of proportions so gigantic as to be almost unbelievable.

She has endured abuse, poverty, weight problems and many ups-and-downs within her career, but has emerged on top without appearing to water down or compromise her own unique style.

Winfrey was born to a teenage mother, who left Winfrey with her grandmother for the first six years of her life. Winfrey's grandmother, although strict, taught Oprah a great deal about literacy and also religion, and Winfrey credits her with many of the successes of her later life. The remainder of Winfrey's childhood was split between her mother in Milwaukee and her father in Tennessee.

Her time with her mother seems to have been unsettled and unsatisfactory and Winfrey has claimed that she was abused by her mother's relatives and friends. In her later high school years with her father, Winfrey was considered gifted and was working on television and radio whilst still studying at Tennessee State University.

Winfrey got her big break while working on morning chat show *AM Chicago*. She took the show from the lowest rated show among its competitors to the highest rated, overtaking her biggest rival in the process. She was then picked up for syndication with her own show by Roger Ebert.

Above: Oprah Winfrey attends the 87th Annual Academy Awards

Left: Oprah Winfrey at "The Immortal Life of Henrietta Lacks" Press Conference

Sport and Entertainment

Her show was called *The Oprah Winfrey Show* and it became a national legend, lasting for 25 years and pulling in some of the biggest audiences for shows of its kind. It was in some ways a new kind of television; it included interviews and celebrities, but had an emotional warmth which included and drew the audience. Winfrey would often become emotionally involved in the stories, in marked contrast to the cold, journalistic interviews presented on other current affairs shows. Through the show, Winfrey herself became a national talking point: her weight and health became subjects for gossip columnists as did her current and past relationships. She revealed the abuse she suffered in childhood as part of a programme about abuse, ushering in a new phenomenon of interviewers becoming personally involved in their own programming. Winfrey's media power was also growing beyond her status as a presenter. She took control of her own television show and also began producing films, including *The Women of Brewster Place* and *Beloved*.

An influence on commercial enterprises also became apparent in Winfrey's work. She began a book club on her TV show and her recommended books often became instant bestsellers; her recommendations on health and fitness made her co-authors, such as fitness guru Bob Green, instantly popular. Her support for Barack Obama may well have influenced his popularity with voters.

Now phenomenally wealthy, Winfrey has aimed to put her money and influence to good use and has become a major philanthropist. Her preferred projects often involve education and support for women and young girls, including the creation of University scholarships in the US and the creation of school places in South Africa. She was awarded the Presidential Medal of Freedom by Barack Obama in 2013.

Right: Oprah Winfrey give the Commencement Address at Agnes Scott College, in 2017, Decatur, Georgia

This is the wonder of Oprah; a rags to riches story of proportions so gigantic as to be almost unbelievable.

Picture Credits

Endpapers:
Getty Images:
Front (l-r) 1 MATT DUNHAM; 2 Hulton Deutsch; 3 David M. Benett; 4 Gerardo Mora; 5 Anne Frank Fonds Basel; 6 Getty Images; 7 Kevin Mazur; 8 Tim Graham; 9 Kelly Kline; 10 Clive Brunskill
Back (l-r) 1 Tim Graham; 2 Bryan Bedder; 3 API; 4 Hulton Archive; 5 Michael Stewart; 6 Roberto Serra / Iguana Press; 7 Hulton Archive; 8 Time Life Pictures; 9 John Lamparski; 10 Spencer Platt
Additional imagery from © iStock/Getty Images

17 © Emma Wesley (the artist)

Getty Images:
4, 141 Library of Congress; 5, 96 Tim Graham; 6, 15 Getty Images; 8 Underwood Archives; 9 Bettmann; 10 Time Life Pictures; 11 Time Life Picture; 12 Bettmann; 13 Boyer/Roger Viollet; 14 Getty Images; 16 Derek Hudson; 19 Universal History Archive; 20-21 View Pictures; 22 Chip Somodevilla; 23 Time Life Pictures; 24 Cynthia Johnson; 25 Bettmann; 26-27 Bettmann; 28 Science & Society Picture Library; 30 Hulton Deutsch; 31 Underwood Archives; 34-35 Education Images; 36 Jack Taylor; 37 Jack Taylor; 38 Baron; 39 Bettmann; 40-41 Fox Photos; 42, 65t Nomi Ellenson; 45 Hulton Archive; 46 Hulton Archive; 49t Roland Schoor, 49bl George Hoyningen-Huene/RDA, 49br Edward Berthelot; 50 Ebet Roberts; 51 Keystone; 52 Anne Frank Fonds Basel; 54-55 Anne Frank Fonds Basel; 56 Nick Harvey; 59 Jeff J Mitchell; 60 Roberto Serra / Iguana Press; 61 Bettmann; 62 Bettmann; 63 Bettmann; 64 David M. Benett; 65b Jon Furniss; 66, 99 Gemma Levine; 68 Topical Press Agency; 69 ullstein bild Dtl.; 70 George Rinhart; 71 IWM/Getty Images; 72 Anwar Hussein; 73 Jean-Claude FRANCOLON; 74 Tim Graham; 75 michel Setboun; 76 UniversalImagesGroup; 77 UniversalImagesGroup; 78 Kean Collection; 79 Bettmann; 80 Bloomberg; 81 Anadolu Agency; 82 Barbara Akoer; 84 Bettmann; 85 Jack Sotomayor; 87 Time Life Pictures; 88-89 Hulton Archive; 91 Photo 12; 92 PAUL SANCYA; 93 Don Cravens; 95 Keystone-France; 97 Tim Graham; 98 Princess Diana Archive; 101 Underwood Archives; 102 MATT DUNHAM; 103 TONY KARUMBA; 104, 145 Tim Graham; 107 Allison Shelley; 108 Allison Shelley; 109t Justin Sullivan, 109b Marla Aufmuth; 111 J. Wilds; 112 Eric BOUVET; 113 Derek Hudson; 115 Chip HIRES; 116 DEA / S. VANNINI; 117 API; 118 Monica Schipper; 119 Daniel Zuchnik; 120-121 John Lamparski; 122 Tim Graham; 123 Imagno; 124 John Moore; 125 Thos Robinson; 126 Spencer Platt; 127 Chip Somodevilla; 128 NurPhoto; 129 Chesnot; 130 Ulrich Baumgarten; 131 Michele Tantussi; 132 Alex Wong; 133 Bryan Bedder; 134 Gerardo Mora; 135t Chip Somodevilla, 135b CHRIS KLEPONIS; 137 Keystone; 138 Hulton Archive; 140 Fotosearch; 142 Peter Macdiarmid; 143 Bettmann; 144 Jean GUICHARD; 150, 172 Vera Anderson; 152 Hulton Archive; 153 Hulton Archive; 154 Bettmann; 155 Hulton Archive; 157 Alfred Eisenstaedt; 158 Kelly Kline; 160 Jamie McCarthy; 161 Alex Goodlett; 163 Barcroft Media; 164 Michael Ochs Archives; 165 Michael Ochs Archives; 166 Edward Miller; 167 Gilles Petard; 168 Michael Stewart; 171 Clive Brunskill; 173 Kevin Mazur; 175 Rick Diamond

© iStock/Getty Images:
7; 20, 58; 32; 43; 67; 86; 105; 146; 147; 148-149; 151; 174